ABORTION IS GOOD FOR AMERICA

--AND THE WORLD

WHY THE OPPOSITION?

Dr. Bob O'Connor

Total Health Publications

2020

THERE ARE NO SOCIETAL REASONS TO FORBID ABORTIONS.

➤ Allowing abortion reduces taxes (for education, health care such as Medicaid, welfare payments, and judicial and prison expenses),

➤ More children contribute to overpopulation and climate change,

➤ Climate change, with global warming, increases famines and decreases fresh water,

➤ Disallowing abortion increases the unhappiness of women who do not want a child at that time,

➤ Not allowing it decreases the contributions to society of women who want to further their education,

➤ Forbidding it increases the number of unwanted and abused children,

➤ More abused children increase the amount of criminal and other anti-social behavior.

CHAPTER ONE

WHY THE OPPOSITION TO ABORTION IN THE UNITED STATES?

TRADITION

What we learned at mother's knee—or some other joint, is fundamental to our belief system. We seldom think our way into our beliefs, we merely accept what we have been told by our parents, priests, and neighbors.

Traditions can be valuable, like looking both ways before you cross a street. But they can also be counterproductive, like protecting coal mining when there are cheaper and cleaner methods of producing electricity.

Abortion is not proscribed in the Bible. In fact, it is quite clear that life begins with the first breath—not at conception or with the first heartbeat! The Jews, because they read the Scriptures, are well aware of this fact. According to Religion News Service, in a survey done in 2016, only 20% of Christians had read the whole Bible, while over 50% had not read any part, or had read only a few stories.

Still, the United States is apparently a very religious country. In an international survey measuring the importance of religion in one's everyday life, 70%believed that religion was important in their lived. This compared with Estonia, the Scandinavian countries, and most of Europe which were significantly less religious. These less religious countries had only 15 to 20% of their populations that found religion important in their lives. At the other end of the scale, Somalia, Bangladesh, and Ethiopia had 100% of their populations who believed deeply in their religions.

TRADITIONS, RELIGIOUS BELIEFS, AND EDUCATION

Traditions are like matter, which according to Newton's laws of motion, remains at rest until moved. When moved, an equal and opposite force is exerted against the moving force. From an intellectual point of view, we can expect opposition to the long-held view that abortion is illegal, because at the beginning of the 20th century abortion was outlawed in most countries.

Historically, religion sanctifies what society is already doing. When Moses descended Mt. Sinai with his Ten Commandments, society had already decided that murder, stealing, adultery, and bearing false witness were bad for society, and that there was a god above the society. The Babylonian king, Hammurabi, had already spelled it out, in far more detail, a thousand years earlier.

So, looking at the needs of American society 100 years ago we can see how abortion might not be desirable—so this societal need might be championed by the various religions.

At that time, in 1900, the life expectancy for men was 41. We were in a period where the economic system was based on physical labor. Today, by contrast, the male life expectancy is 79 and the economic system is highly intellectually intensive—so the worker can work more years. Consequently, we don't need as many workers. And those we need require much more education. Also, few women worked in 1900, today most women do. Additionally, computers, robotics, 3d printing, and artificial intelligence make every worker more productive.

As the methods of aborting have become incredibly safe, abortion is much safer than giving birth. The freedom of women to attend universities and to enter the labor force gives women more choice in choosing relationships and motherhood. This has been very important in reversing traditions in most of the Western world. 98% of countries allow abortion to save the life of the mother. 63% of countries allow it to preserve the mental health pf the pregnant woman. 43% allow it in the case of rape or incest. 39% allow it if the infant is to be severely impaired. 33% allow abortion for economic or social reasons. 27% allow it when requested by the woman.

The developing countries are much less likely to allow abortions than are the developed countries.

CHAPTER TWO

A Pew report, surveying over 35,000 people found that 45% of Christians seldom or never read the Bible, but 35% read it at least once a week. The sects with the highest level of readers were: Jehovah's Witnesses, Mormons, Evangelicals, and the historically Black Protestants. These were in the 60 to 85% ranges. Catholics and mainline Protestants were 30% or less. It might also be noted that the less the educational level, the more likely that the person would be: a Bible-reader, believe that it was the word of God, and that abortion and homosexuality should be prohibited.

The survey did not indicate whether the Bible was read in its entirety or whether it was understood-- or whether the beliefs of the readers came from their ministers and priests.

If people have read and understood the Bible, these following citations will not be new, but for those who believe that the Bible is the word of God, and literally true, these passages should be internalized when deciding on a religious proscription against abortion.

LIFE STARTS WITH THE FIRST BREATH

THE BIBLE

The Bible is generally clear that life starts with the first breath. the Jewish tradition has followed this idea since it was introduced. Jeremiah did enunciate a contrary view, but it was definitely a minority view, compared to the writings of Moses. in Genesis 2:7 it is written that, "then the Lord God formed man of dust from the ground, and breathed into his nostrils the breath of life; and man became a living being."

ABORTION IS REQUIRED IN THE BIBLE IN AT LEAST ONE CIRCUMSTANCE

In Numbers 5:11, the Lord spoke to Moses about what should be the priest's duty when a woman has been accused of adultery. She is given "bitter water" to cause an abortion. In verses 21 and 22 it says when the priest is to put the woman under this curse—"may the LORD cause you to become a curse among your people when he makes your womb miscarry and your abdomen swell. May this water that brings a curse enter your body so that your abdomen swells or your womb miscarries." So, according to what God told Moses, abortion is required of a woman is pregnant from an adulterous relationship. In fact, it is part of the "curse" of her misdeed.

American laws that disallow abortions for rape, incest, and adultery would seem to be diametrically opposed to what God told Moses.

On the other hand, nowhere does the Bible say that it is not allowed in cases where it is voluntary. As Moses mentioned, there was at least one abortifacient that was known in those early times.

Hosea (9:14) tells us that part of the punishment for not being faithful to the God of Israel is that "wombs that miscarry and breasts that are dry." So God will cause the spontaneous abortions.

THE FETUS NOT A PERSON—AND IS NOT SACRED

In Deuteronomy 28:18, God warns the Israelites that they must keep his Commandments. He cites the benefits of following them and the evils of disobedience. Among the evils are that: "The fruit of your womb will be cursed, and the crops of your land, and the calves of your herds and the lambs of your flocks.

Ripping open pregnant women is allowed by God for disobedience to Him, but it is also prevalent in wars, which He could control if He so desired.

God will punish the Israelites by destroying their unborn children, who will die at birth, or perish in the womb, or never even be conceived. (Hosea 9:10-16)

Even Jesus, in commenting on the approaching end of the world, thought not of sparing pregnant or nursing women. In Matthew 24:19 he said, "Woe to pregnant women and those who are nursing." So the often merciless God of the Old Testament may not be dead!

A FETUS IS NOT YET A PERSON—ONLY THE PROPERTY OF THE HUSBAND

EXODUS 21:22-25 "If people are fighting and hit a pregnant woman and she gives birth prematurely but there is no serious injury, the offender must be fined whatever the woman's husband demands and the court allows. But if there is serious injury, you are to take life for life, eye for eye, tooth for tooth, hand for hand, foot for foot, burn for burn, wound for wound, bruise for bruise."

GOD IS NOT PRO-LIFE

The killing of all people, including fetuses and children in Sodom and Gomorrah, is but one of about two dozen of such God caused mass extinctions. God certainly directed David's shot that killed Goliath. And in Jeremiah 44:7-8 It is said about worshipping other gods: "Now this is what the LORD God Almighty, the God of Israel, says: Why bring such great disaster on yourselves by cutting off from Judah the men and women, the children and infants, and so leave yourselves without a remnant? Why arouse my anger with what your hands have made . . ."

In 2 Samuel 11, we have the account of David seeing the beautiful Bathsheba, whom he had been told was married. He slept with her in an adulterous affair and she became pregnant. So David put her husband, Uriah, in the front of the ranks where he was certain to be killed—and he was. (Verses 14-17) Then Bathsheba became David's wife. So David was involved in an adulterous affair-- a capital crime. "If a man commits adultery with another man's wife—with the wife of his neighbor—both the adulterer and the adulteress are to be put to death." (Leviticus 20:10) It is echoed in Deuteronomy 22:22, "If a man is found sleeping with another man's wife, both the man who slept with her and the woman must die. You must purge the evil from Israel."

And it might be said that David planned the killing of Uriah. 2 Samuel 11:27, but that conspiracy is not clearly a Biblical sin, as it is in federal law where conspiracy to commit murder can bring up to life imprisonment.

Still, we are told that "the Lord was displeased with him." Perhaps it is like today where crimes by people in high places are not as severely punished as those committed by people farther down the pecking order!

SHOULD CHRISTIANS SPEND MORE TIME ADVOCATING WHAT THE BIBLE HAS ACTUALLY APPROVED?

SLAVERY

One would expect that because of the Israelites enslavement in Egypt, that the message of the Bible would be totally anti-slavery. However, one finds strong pro- and anti-slavery positions in both the Old and the New testaments. A few of the many references follow:

Leviticus 25:44-46--"As for your male and female slaves whom you may have: you may buy male and female slaves from among the nations that are around you. You may also buy from among the strangers who sojourn with you and their clans that are with you, who have been born in your land, and they may be your property. You may bequeath them to your sons after you to inherit as a possession forever. You may make slaves of them, but over your brothers the people of Israel you shall not rule, one over another ruthlessly."

Exodus 21:20-21 --"If a man strikes his slave, male or female, with a rod and the slave dies under his hand, he shall be avenged. But if the slave survives a day or two, he is not to be avenged, for the slave is his money."

Exodus 21:26-27 --"When a man strikes the eye of his slave, male or female, and destroys it, he shall let the slave go free because of his eye. If he knocks out the tooth of his slave, male or female, he shall let the slave go free because of his tooth."

Exodus 21:2 --"When you buy a Hebrew slave, he shall serve six years, and in the seventh he shall go out free, for nothing."

And from the new Testament:

Colossians 4:1 --"Masters, treat your slaves justly and fairly, knowing that you also have a Master in heaven."

Ephesians 6:5 –"Slaves, obey your earthly masters with fear and trembling, with a sincere heart, as you would Christ,"

Titus 2:9-10 –"Slaves are to be submissive to their own masters in everything; they are to be well-pleasing, not argumentative, not pilfering, but showing all good faith, so that in everything they may adorn the doctrine of God our Savior."

1 Timothy 6:1-2 "Let all who are under a yoke as slaves regard their own masters as worthy of all honor, so that the name of God and the teaching may not be reviled. Those who have believing masters must not be disrespectful on the ground that they are brothers; rather they must serve all the better since those who benefit by their good service are believers and beloved. Teach and urge these things."

CAPITAL PUNISHMENT

The worst offense in the Bible is worshipping a false god. This is mentioned over 300 times and it carried the death penalty. Blasphemy is a similarly nasty offense. Adultery is sometimes a capital offense (Leviticus 20:10), as is murder (Leviticus 24:17) and sometimes rape.

ADVOCATING THE APPROVED PRACTICES OF THE BIBLE

It would appear that if the message of the Bible is primary in some people's lives, that they should spend their time advocating and legislating for propositions actually found in the Bible—such as advocating slavery and capital punishment.

The anti-abortion legislatures tend to be for capital punishment for murder, as the Bible teaches. But perhaps they should also work to legislate capital punishment for blasphemy and adultery. We might assume that there are too many people shouting "Jesus Christ" when they are angry at things, or "God damn you" when they are angry at people. Shouldn't they be stoned?

As long as we have a nominal separation of church and state it would be unwise to seek to reinstall slavery as an economic tool. In fact, it isn't needed now with automation, artificial intelligence, robots, and 3D printing. And, of course, it would require a Constitutional amendment to invalidate the 13th Amendment.

AND ANOTHER THEOLOGICAL QUESTION!

Anti-abortion zealots assert that human life begins at conception, and therefore the fertilized egg possesses all constitutional rights of a living person. It follows that destruction of a conceived embryo (blastocyst) is murder. This is the basis for the "personhood" argument which has been defeated in five statewide initiatives since 2010.

The Bible declares that God breathed life into man's body (Genesis 2:7). At least a dozen more verses indicate that breath is synonymous with life. This scriptural truth completely contradicts the personhood dogma.

More importantly, if the fertilized ovum is a person, as anti-abortion extremists claim, then God's record as the greatest murderer of unborn children is expanded further. That is because most fertilized eggs either fail to implant in the uterine wall and pass out of the body, or they do implant, begin to develop and then are spontaneously aborted. Fewer than one-third of fertilized ova survive to become living humans.

Why does God murder untold millions of these "persons" every year in the U.S. alone? Why did God, who allegedly loves the unborn and hates abortion, kill so many unborn children, adolescents and adults throughout biblical history? Why do fundamentalists pursue a political agenda that is thoroughly refuted by God's word?

CHAPTER THREE

WHAT DOES FEDERAL LAW SAY?

Aborting an embryo or fetus is not killing a person under Federal law. In the Unborn Victims of Violence Act of 2004, abortion is specifically excluded.

An embryo or fetus does not have rights under Federal law.

As used in this chapter, the term "United States person" means any United States citizen or alien admitted for permanent residence in the United States, and any corporation, partnership, or other organization organized under the laws of the United States.

a) In determining the meaning of any Act of Congress, or of any ruling, regulation, or interpretation of the various administrative bureaus and agencies of the United States, the words "person", "human being", "child", and "individual", shall include every infant member of the species homo sapiens who is born alive at any stage of development.

(b) As used in this section, the term "born alive", with respect to a member of the species homo sapiens, means the complete expulsion or extraction from his or her mother of that member, at any stage of development, who after such expulsion or extraction breathes or has a beating heart, pulsation of the umbilical cord, or definite movement of voluntary muscles, regardless of whether the umbilical cord has been cut, and regardless of whether the expulsion or extraction occurs as a result of natural or induced labor, cesarean section, or induced abortion.

(c) Nothing in this section shall be construed to affirm, deny, expand, or contract any legal status or legal right applicable to any member of the species homo sapiens at any point prior to being "born alive" as defined in this section.

(Added Pub. L. 107–207, § 2(a), Aug. 5, 2002, 116 Stat. 926.)

(Pub. L. 102–484, div. A, title XVII, § 1711, Oct. 23, 1992, 106 Stat. 2581.)

THE LAW TODAY

The US Supreme Court has declared abortion to be a fundamental right guaranteed by the US Constitution. The landmark abortion case Roe v. Wade, decided on January 22, 1973 in favor of abortion rights, remains the law of the land. The 7-2 decision stated that the Constitution gives a guarantee of certain areas or zones of privacy, and that this right of privacy, "is broad enough to encompass a woman's decision whether or not to terminate her pregnancy." The court thoroughly scrutinized the religious and secular history of abortion from the time of the ancient Greeks. It also found that the opinions and laws relative to abortion had become more restrictive in America as the country matured. It disagreed with this regression. In its decision, it also ruled that under the U.S. Constitution the word 'person' does not include the unborn.

RELIGIOUS ADVOCATES FOR CHANGING THE LAW

The Catholic and Mormon religions have championed purely religious reasons to forbid abortion. Joseph Smith, the founder of the Mormon religion was told by an angel that all souls were created at the time of Adam. (Moses 6:8-9) They must be born so that they can be saved and live in heaven. Jeremiah (1:5) backs up this position. "Before I formed thee in the belly I knew thee; and before thou camest forth out of the womb I sanctified thee, and I ordained thee a prophet unto the nations."

The Catholic position is more complicated. The Bible tells us that Adam and Eve sinned by eating the fruit of the Tree of Knowledge. If Bishop Ussher's calculations are correct, this would have been in 4004 BC. Some early Christian writers believed that this sin was inherited by all of us. Baptism was the way to wash away that sin and start living the good life that can get you to heaven.

Mary, the mother of Jesus, must have been perfect from the beginning. Many theologians believed this, then in 1854, Pope Pius IX declared officially that Mary was conceived without Original Sin—her Immaculate Conception. If she was conceived, that must have been the beginning of life and her soul was obviously in existence when she was conceived. So, life must start at conception for everyone. Consequently, in 1869 the same pope decided that all abortions are immoral since all zygotes and embryos have souls.

CHAPTER FOUR

OPINIONS, FACTS, AND EFFECTIVE THINKING

HOW MUCH DO WE EVALUATE THE ISSUES?

WE BELIEVE WHAT WE HEAR

It is puzzling that 60 years ago the evangelical Bible Belt in the Midwest, and the Republican Party, were leading advocates of abortion, The Democrats and Catholics fought it. Now the tides have changed. It goes to show you that if you can repeat a message enough, that many, or most, people will believe it.

America's very low educational rankings seem to indicate that people will believe what they hear the most often. Those that watch CNN will overwhelmingly have different information than those who watch Fox News. Since we develop our opinions based on what we see and hear, if we hear only one side of an argument, we won't be able to make informed decisions.

Whether this has anything to do with education has been a concern. The latest international education scores (PISA—Program for International Student Assessment) in reading, math, and science shows the U.S. ranking 31st of the 70 countries assessed. The countries that were less religious ranked much higher than the U.S. in their educational knowledge. Perhaps the more educated countries have more citizens who have analyzed the facts and the arguments relative to a creating God and a life after death. Perhaps they are more aware of the tragedies caused by a "merciful" Supernatural. Prayer didn't ease the hurricanes of Texas, Florida, and Puerto Rico. It didn't help ISIS to establish a religious state. It didn't stop the child abuse by Catholic priests and Baptist ministers.

The U.S. has 38% of its citizens believing in the idea that God created the world less than 10,000 years ago. Scientific measurements show that it was over 13 billion years ago that the universe was begun—and the God as Creator hypothesis is not a part of it.

DO WE REALLY NEED MORE LABORERS?

Another fact to consider is that fewer people are needed, especially in the laboring force. In 1900, the life expectancy of men at birth was 47 years. For women, it was 49. Now it is 76 for men and 81 for women. How many people are needed with automation doing nearly all the labor-intensive jobs?

Retirement at 65 or 67 is another factor. In 1936, when Social Security was begun, retirement was at 65 while the life expectancy was 64. The government made money. The government uses the contributions as part of their annual income. While the government officially "borrows" the money, it is a very large part of the U.S. government's $2.5 trillion national debt—the world's largest. The problem is that pensions must be paid with each succeeding budget—and the amount due increases yearly.

People are used to the tradition of retiring in the mid-60s. Their Social Security contributions are used up in 5 to 7 years, but they live another 15. (Life expectancy at birth is near 80, but those who live to 65 can expect another 20.5 years.) The government isn't used to this! So, let's encourage more births and outlaw abortions so that these eventual workers will help to pay for the benefits of those who are retired.

The obvious problem is that if we need 5 to 7 new workers to support a retiree now, we will need 26 to 50 to support those 5 to 7 when they retire in 45 years. Then in another 40 or 50 years we will need another 150 to 250 to support them.

The obvious solutions would be to increase the required payroll taxes that pay for retirement, or raise the retirement age—or both! But in our democratic republic how many legislators would be re-elected if they voted against our traditional retirement expectations? So, let's outlaw abortions to produce more workers!

AND WHAT ABOUT THE PLANET'S MAJOR PROBLEM--OVERPOPULATION?

The major concern we hear the most seems to be—how will we feed them. But perhaps there are other concerns. How will they be educated? Where will the new jobs appear—with robots, computers, 3D printing, and artificial intelligence doing the traditional jobs. One solution might be a world-wide emphasis on contraceptives and abortion. But NO! That would go against our religious and secular traditions!

INTERNATIONAL HUMAN RIGHTS STATEMENTS

National and international organizations have advocated family-planning for a number of years. They have also called for both more freedom and equality in making one's own decisions on how and where to live. These are often antithetical aspirations.

When one has a number of children, such as in Mali where the fertility rate is 7, the status of the mother or father may be enhanced with a large family, or they are praised by their religious leaders. So, reducing the average family size is more than difficult.

RELIGIOUS BELIEFS CAN INTERFERE WITH SOCIAL REALITIES

Just look at the Dugger family in Arkansas. This highly religious family with 19 children, all home-schooled and none college educated, has been praised in America and rewarded with a reality TV show that paid them at least $25,000 per episode until it was cancelled because it was revealed that one of the boys had molested several girls when he was a teenager.

The Biblical command in the Garden of Eden to "be fruitful and multiply and replenish the earth" was issued when there were only two people on earth, Adam and Eve. The question is whether since the earth is now more "replenished" than it has ever been, does that command tell us now to stop replenishing? Is it even possible that multiplying once the earth is replenished a sin because it exceeds God's command?

DECLARATIONS OF HUMAN RIGHTS

Internationally we have some major pronouncements such as the United Nations' 1948 Universal Declaration of Human Rights, and their 1966 International Covenant on Civil and Political Rights. In Europe, we have the European Convention on Human Rights and Fundamental Freedoms. Each guarantees the rights of women. The UN also clearly states that the child has rights after being born. Some women have successfully used these lists of rights in courts to counter religious arguments against abortion.

The European Convention, enforced by the European Court of Justice, has made some decisions regarding equal rights that are not only upsetting to the countries' courts that were overruled, but may play a part in countries considering leaving the EU.

Two such decisions were somewhat influential in the United Kingdom's decision to leave the European Union. The UK wanted to make its own decisions of what was best for them. One such case involved a violent Islamic terrorist that the EU did not want to allow to return. The other involved a murderer who had stomped a man do death because he would not give him a cigarette. While serving his life sentence, he married a female prisoner. They wanted a child, the British courts said "no." One might expect that with two criminal parents, one a sadistic murderer, the child might not have an ideal family life. Along with this, it is highly likely that the child would be raised on the meager welfare payments from the state. But human rights prevail over the needs of a society!

In Africa, the Maputo Protocol (The Protocol to the African Charter on Human and Peoples' Rights on the Rights of Women in Africa) is legally binding on the 37 countries that have ratified it. Included in it is the elimination of genital mutilation and the right to political equality for women. It also allowed abortion "in cases of sexual assault, rape, incest, and where the continued pregnancy endangers the mental and physical health of the mother or the life of the mother or the fetus." A year later, in 2017, African leaders went further, viewing abortion as a human right. There has been opposition by the Catholics to the abortion legalization, and by some Muslim countries to the outlawing of "female circumcision,"

WHAT DO THE LATEST ABORTION LAWS PROTECT?

Human life begins:

➤ Life beginning at conception: Alabama

➤ Life as beginning with the fetal heartbeat, at about six weeks is protected in: Louisiana, Georgia, Ohio, Kentucky, Mississippi

➤ After 8 weeks in: Missouri

➤ 18 weeks: Utah

Other factors:

➤ No exception for rape or incest: Louisiana, Missouri, Alabama, Ohio

➤ Exceptions: life of the mother Louisiana, Alabama, Georgia, Utah

➤ Severe deformity to child (medically futile): Louisiana

➤ Parental approval required: Missouri

These laws were passed with generally huge majorities:

➤ The Louisiana law passed the legislative houses by 79-23 and 31-5 majorities.

➤ The Missouri law passed 110-44 and 24-10

➤ The Alabama law passed 74-3 and 25-6

➤ Ohio 56-39 and 18-15

➤ Utah (Senate vote 23-6)

Some might wonder why this obviously religious anti-abortion idea is not mentioned in the Bible. It is also not against Federal law.

I guess, that if I believe it--it doesn't have to be in the Bible. God obviously forgot to include it.

The Mormons believe that all souls were created with the creation of the world. Plato had believed something like this—there was a pre-existence of one's self and some of what had been learned in a prior life was known when we are born. Origen, one of the early Church fathers believed it also. But in the Second Council of Constantinople, in 553, by a "democratic" vote decided that Origen's ideas were false. The all-knowing prelates chose not to believe Jeremiah. So the idea was lost until Joseph Smith revived it.

PENALTIES FOR THOSE WHO AID IN ABORTIONS

The penalty for doctors who are abortion providers in Alabama is 10 to 99 years in prison. However, the greatest number of abortions, estimated at 20,000 to 30,000 per year, are the spontaneous abortions, also termed miscarriages, that are caused by God.

To be fair, God should be punished at least as stringently as physicians who perform abortions. Since it is useless to subpoena God, perhaps the churches that worship Him should be closed. This would include Catholic, Baptist, and many other such churches. That might make Him think twice!

ANTI-ABORTION LAWS RECENTLY DEFEATED

Delaware and Florida have defeated stronger abortion laws. Other states are passing, or thinking of passing, more lenient abortion laws. Someday the U.S. may equal its neighbor to the north in allowing abortions on demand.

New York allows abortions even if Roe v. Wade is overturned. The vote was 92-42 in the Assembly and 38-24 in the Senate.

Vermont and Illinois are considering abortion a fundamental right. Expanded rights to abortion are also being considered in: Rhode Island, Maine, Nevada, and Hawaii.

DOES EDUCATION, OR THE LACK OF IT, PLAY A PART?

We can look for a number of reasons for certain states to embrace the idea of life starting sometime before birth. One is the education level of the state. US News does a number rankings of schools, colleges, and states. Of the 50 states, Alabama ranks last in education, 50th! New Mexico ranks 49th, Louisiana 48th, Alaska 47th (They are considering the harshest abortion law yet devised.) Mississippi is 46th, Arkansas is 42nd, Kentucky is 38th, Ohio 31st, Georgia 30th, and Missouri 27th.

One might wonder if the low levels of educational achievement might be a factor in their not evaluating all of the options in any serious political question.

The US News rankings of state universities is somewhat similar, but some states do somewhat better with their universities, but their tuition levels may prohibit many students from attending. The ranking and tuition levels according to the US News rankings are:

➤ Alabama rankings 115 and 129 ($11,000 in state tuition)
➤ Louisiana 140 ($10,000 to $12,000)
➤ Mississippi 152 ($9,000)
➤ Arkansas 152 (tie) ($9,000)
➤ Ohio 56 ($11,000)
➤ Georgia 46 ($12,000)
➤ Missouri 129 ($10,000)

YOUNG UNEDUCATED MOTHERS IN ALABAMA

Alabama's pregnancy rate per 1,000 girls aged 15-19 is 40.1. And their teen birth rate is 20.7 per 1000 girls. Does this have anything to do with their dismal education performance?

The Alabama pregnancy rate is higher than the U.S. average and its abortion rate is below the U.S. average. So the state has a very high number of very young mothers. We can assume that they are not highly educated. It is conceivable that the children will not grow up in an enriched environment.

WHO IS RIGHT ON THIS ISSUE OF ABORTION?

Matthew 18:18-20 tells us that, "Truly I tell you, whatever you bind on earth will be bound in heaven, and whatever you loose on earth will be loosed in heaven. . . Again, truly I tell you that if two of you on earth agree about anything they ask for, it will be done for them by my Father in heaven. For where two or three gather in my name, there am I with them."

So, if two or three Christians agree on an issue, God will accept it. Therefore, both advocating and prohibiting abortions are approved by God—as long as the proponents on both sides are Christians. This is necessary because God forgot to mention this practice specifically in His Bible.

IT IS ABOUT TRADITION

By the beginning of the 20th century, abortion was illegal or severely restricted in most countries. The restrictions were either from common law, as in the UK and its possessions, civil law as in other European countries and their possessions, or Islamic law, which was used by some Islamic countries. Where it was outlawed, it was usually because of: danger to the mother from unlicensed abortionists; it was a sin and the laws were geared to punish the sinner; or often, the life of the fetus was considered important.

BUT NEW LAWS CHANGE OUR TRADITIONS

While abortion was criminalized in England in 1861, it was modified in 1967 and in 1990. Ireland had a very restrictive policy, seeing the same value of life of the mother as that of the fetus. But as of 2019, after a referendum, abortion is now allowed in a number of situations.

Today abortion is legally permitted to save the life of the woman in 98% of world's countries. 63% of countries allow it to preserve the physical or mental health of the woman. 43% allow it in the case of rape or incest. 39% allow it if the infant is to be severely impaired. 33% allow abortion for economic or social reasons. 27% allow it when requested by the woman. The developing countries are much less likely to allow abortions than are the developed countries.

But now abortion methods have become incredibly safe, if done by competent people.

In recent decades in Latin America, a combination of legislation and judicial review has lessened the resictions to abortion.

CHAPTER FIVE
POSITIVES FOR SOCIETY

There are a several major reasons for society to allow or even encourage abortions. One is to be able to limit populations that are overcrowded. Another is to protect children from being born into homes that don't want them. The financial cost to society of unwanted children goes beyond the normal societal expenses of educating their young future citizens, it often includes expenses for orphanages, increased expenses for rehabilitation from physical and mental abuse, drug rehabilitation, and increased expenses for police, judicial procedures, and prisons. (Federal prisons cost $35,000 per year per prisoner. This compares with $70,000 in California and New York and $15,000 in Alabama.) So, if people want lower taxes, abortion is a major way to reduce them.

We now know, from epigenetic research, that abused and neglected children often have changes to their genes and brains that increase their likelihood of becoming violent. Irregularities in the brain's pre-frontal cortex, or areas around the hypothalamus (such as the limbic system or amygdala) can predict violence.

The MAOA (the so-called warrior gene) is one of more than 50 genes that can be influenced epigenetically. The behavioral changes can range from problems with impulse control to the inability to control violent behavior. A classic study in Finland found that such epigenetic residues were found only in violent prisoners, not in the non-violent ones. As a result of the study, it was predicted that 5 to 10% of violent crime in Finland was a result of genetic and epigenetic causes.

Brain research continues to uncover causes of behavior that are related to epigenetic changes. For example, recent research has found that at least one cause of autism is caused by first trimester epigenetic changes to the MEMO1 gene on the second chromosome. Epilepsy can also be influenced by this gene which is responsible for the development of important brain cells.

This is also true of neurotransmitter activity--with increases of dopamine or decreases in serotonin. These changes begin in the intra-uterine environment and accumulate through life if stresses persist. Such stresses can include: a pregnant mother who is unhappy, or on legal and illegal drugs. After birth, the child's negative epigenetic changes an come from being bullied, being neglected, physical or sexual abuse, etc.

A society might require that fetuses which are likely to be unloved, abused, or neglected be aborted. The costs of the potentially unloved children in terms of societal problems range well beyond the financial.

FINANCIAL REASONS

Abortion reduces welfare costs to taxpayers. The Congressional Budget Office evaluated a proposed anti-abortion bill that would ban all abortions nationwide after 20 weeks of pregnancy, and found that the resulting additional births would increase the federal deficit by $225 million over nine years--due to the increased need for Medicaid coverage. Also, since many women seeking late-term abortions are economically disadvantaged, their children are likely to require welfare assistance.

Every child, wanted or unwanted, costs about $120,000 if they go to public schools. Then there are the significant police, judicial, and prison expenses for those who go wrong. The average cost of incarcerating a juvenile who has run afoul of the law is $112,000 per year.

The cost of an abortion can be free for impoverished women from some clinics, such as Planned Parenthood. Other physician performed procedures usually cost between $300 during the first trimester to $3,000 during the second trimester. Most are paid by the woman, but even if the government paid for them all, it would be far ahead financially since it would not have to pay the education or other expenses that many children and adults require of the government.

Then there is the probable economic advantage that if the women who did not want children were to stay in the work force or in higher education, the society would profit--especially if they work at the higher-level jobs.

TAXATION

While the U.S. has a relatively low taxation rate, by developed country standards (about 28% for all taxes, compared with the 40+% in Europe), the citizenry continually complains about their high taxes. Allowing for abortions will substantially reduce the need for taxes in many areas, such as: education, Medicaid, prisons, police, welfare, etc.) For example:

In 2015, Alabama had 5900 legal abortions.

Georgia 2000

Ohio 21000

Missouri 4800

Louisiana 9400

Texas 54,000

Utah 3,000

The education tax dollars saved in these 7 states for 2015 totaled $12 billion. Texas saved $650,000,000 in education expenses, in 2017, from the abortions performed.

For the 638,000 abortions performed in the U.S. that year, the savings in primary and secondary education dollars was in excess of $76 billion. This would be enough to give every one of the 20 million college students $3800 every year. Or if based on need, far more than that for the poorer students.

THE WORLD IS OVERPOPULATED

Every child, wanted or unwanted, contributes to the world's overpopulation. Overpopulation is the planet's major problem. It is responsible for climate change and many other societal problems, like wars and terrorism, plastics in the ocean, over-fishing, garbage disposal problems, the lack of potable water, and a host of other problems.

The population now is over seven and a half billion people, most of whom live in the cities. According to Professor Emeritus David Pimentel, of Cornell University—the major authority on overpopulation, if all people are to live at the same standards as found in the developed countries in the West, one to one and a half billion would be the planet's maximum capacity.

City living is usually accompanied by the greater use of concrete for buildings and roads. Concrete production produces 5 to 8% of CO_2 emissions—second only to fossil fuel burning. Concrete and asphalt in buildings and roads often cover topsoil that is necessary for growing crops, so agriculture is impaired. Then when rains come, since there is less ground to absorb the water, heavy runoff or floods carry away some of the topsoil. Dr. Pimentel believes that this soil erosion is the second biggest problem for our world—after overpopulation.

FEWER PEOPLE WILL REDUCE THE GREENHOUSE GASES THAT CREATE GLOBAL WARMING AND CLIMATE CHANGE

The average person in a developed country adds about 5,000 tons of carbon dioxide to the atmosphere. To this is added methane and other greenhouse gases that result from living in an advanced society. If the person eats beef, other meats, or eggs—or drinks milk—much more methane is added to the atmosphere. And methane is more damaging than carbon dioxide. Additionally, the progeny of that unwanted child will each contribute to the problem.

According to the United Nations, in the last twenty years, 91% of natural disasters were caused by climate change, due to greenhouse gases. These disasters include: wildfires, droughts, floods, hurricanes, tornadoes, heat waves, famines, and excessive rain and snow storms. The cost of these was $2.25 trillion.

FEWER PEOPLE EASES THE NEED FOR FRESH WATER FOR PERSONAL NEEDS AND FOOD PRODUCTION

There is a great deal of water on the earth—most of it is unusable salt water. Some of the fresh water is frozen in ice sheets and glaciers. Much of fresh water is not potable (drinkable). Only about 0.003% of water is potable. Much of that is used in agriculture.

Both non-potable fresh water and sea water can be made drinkable—but it is very expensive. Some cities, like Los Angeles, are working on making sewage water potable. Los Angeles County has some areas where they use "gray water" (partially treated water) in some agricultural situations.

FREEDOM FOR THE CITIZENS TO CHOSE THE WAY TO LIVE THEIR LIVES

The Roe v. Wade decision affirmed this freedom as Constitutionally required. But some pseudo-religious people believe that abortion is frowned on by God. The evidence herein presented shows that God even requires abortion in some situations.

REDUCTION IN CRIME

Abortion reduces crime. According to a study co-written in 2001, by Freakonomics co-author Steven D. Levitt, PhD, of the University of Chicago, and John Donahue of Yale, and published in the peer-reviewed Quarterly Journal of Economics, legalized abortion has contributed significantly to recent crime reductions. About 18 years after abortion was legalized, crime rates dropped significantly. It was also found that crime rates dropped earlier in states that had previously allowed abortion. Poorer women in areas of high crime rates might also be quite likely to avail themselves of abortion.

Studies in Canada and Australia found the same thing. Some critics mention that the drop in crack cocaine use or better policing techniques might also explain the findings. But these uncorroborated ideas have also been criticized.

SEPARATION OF CHURCH AND STATE

It seems that even when we have the theoretical separation between church and state, the church's theology may remain in the minds of the judges and legislators. Even atheists often carry religious assumptions with them from childhood or from the community. But fetuses have not always been so protected.

Historically, late term fetuses, or even infants, have not escaped the possibility that they won't see tomorrow. Subsistence economies often can't provide for every "product of passion" that pops into their financially limited world. Some societies see no need to nurture those infants who are unlikely to strongly wield a scythe or a sword for several years. When the physical is more important than the spiritual, any manner of eugenic devices may be allowed or encouraged. Therefore, infanticide has often been the necessary action. Luckily, today, contraception and abortion are more generally available—and are certainly preferable to killing a newborn. But as we know, unwanted babies often are found in trash cans.

Whatever the issue—abortion, gun control, free speech, marijuana legalization, climate change, or any of the pressing issues for American and the world—we must look to facts and logic for the best chance at understanding the problem and solving it. Mere opinions, based on traditions or wishes, murky that waters that must be clear.

Legislators, judges, and the rest of us, are often tethered to traditions or imprisoned by our opinions. And we are often influenced by the loudest voice in the room.

OUR FREEDOM OF SPEECH IDEAS

For example, in the freedom of speech area, the original intent was to allow the expression of well thought-out political opinions, no matter how contrary they might be to prevailing thought. Our Supreme Court has limited such speech during wartime and for communists advocating the overthrow of the government. And, God knows that the Founding Fathers had no intention to violently overthrow the government of King George!

But the Court in Brandenburg v. Ohio, in 1969, astonished a few people. At a Ku Klux Klan meeting in Brandenburg, rural Ohio, one of the speeches referred to "revengeance" against "niggers", "Jews", and those who supported them. (If "revengeance" doesn't sound like a word to you, it really isn't—but you can believe that it has a powerful meaning to some uneducated white Christians with huge inferiority feelings. And the mantra that "we is better than them," is an easy way to develop the feeling of power that insecure people need.)

The Court changed its emphasis on what is not allowed as free speech from being "a bad tendency," as in its earlier cases to an "imminent lawless action, that is likely to incite and produce such lawless action." So it would appear that as long as you don't say "let's kill them NOW," and leave it to the audience as to whether killing them tomorrow will be soon enough, it appears that your speech is protected!

AND GUN CONTROL

Similarly, the recent change in the Second Amendment's original meaning of "A well-regulated militia being necessary, the right to bear arms shall not be infringed," has had its original meaning changed both philosophically and grammatically by the Court.

So, while the right to own guns, for most people, is the law of the land, it has only been true since the decisions made in 2008 and 2010. One might suspect that the writers of the Constitution would disagree with the recent court decisions—at least if we can believe Founding Father James Madison's essay in Federalist Papers, Number 46. He tells us of the intention of the "right to bear arms" phrase. It was all about a national guard to protect the nation. It wasn't about hunting or self-defense. But why are we paying Supreme Court Justices if it isn't to change the meaning of the Constitution? At least it keeps them off the welfare rolls!

AND BACK TO ABORTION

There are no religious or societal reasons for not applauding the abortions of unwanted children. The opposition to abortions comes from:

➤ Religious sects that want more members,

➤ Business people who want more customers,

➤ Politicians who want more soldiers, and

➤ People who want to continue their local traditions.

These desires are generally couched in religious suppositions that may, or may not, be based on their scriptures. But even if based on scriptures, rather than facts—they are in the areas of the non-provable—that is why "faith" is essential. And it seems that in America, faith is generally more important than facts. The legislators and courts generally bend over backwards to protect opinions, or beliefs, no matter how anti-social they may be.

DO YOU THINK THAT FACTS, RATHER THAN FAITH, MIGHT BE THE BASES OF BETTER LAWS AND COURT DECISIONS?

APPENDIX

It is not enough to look at some of the social reasons that abortion is an essential answer to many of the national and the world problems. Overpopulation has been consistently listed as the planet's number one problem. Climate change is our second biggest problem.

When we look at reducing climate change we cite: developing renewable energy as the major need. But we seldom cite the major problem—there are too many people using fossil fuels. We can add to that the plastic pollution of the oceans, the expected climate migrations in a few years due to unbearable heat in countries near the equator, to the rise of ocean levels wiping out island nations and threatening coastal cities. (For more on this, read the free e-book "Extinction Rebellion."

But there is so much more. Many excess children in Africa and India are sold as slaves, abandoned to the streets, or merely killed. Probably the greatest problem of all is the number of children born to parents who are not capable of loving. This brings us the candidates for jihadism, street gangs, and criminality in general.

So to add to the text on abortion, we should venture a bit farther into some areas we touched on in the text. But be warned—we will question the "human right" of all people to have children, unless they can effectively raise them!

OVERPOPULATION—THE ELEPHANT IN THE ROOM

DON'T READ THIS APPENDIX IF YOU ARE BOUND BY TRADITIONS

OVERPOPULATION—THE MAJOR FACTOR IN CLIMATE CHANGE

These are very long chapters that merely scratch the surface of the many problems related to our present state of overpopulation and to the number of problems that will occur if the number of people are reduced to a sustainable population level. The suggested level is less than 2 billion according to Dr. David Pimentel, Professor Emeritus of Cornell University, probably the world's foremost authority on the issue. The 2 million number assumes that all people on the planet will live at the standards that the West enjoys.

As in any area where suggestions are made, the possibilities must be explored. It is not enough to cay "cut carbon dioxide emissions," we must suggest how it can be done most effectively and with the least disruption to the society. Reducing the population has many negatives, such as: religious objections, the economic interests of manufacturers for an ever-increasing customer-base, and the government's professed need for more soldiers—even though the next big war will be fought with drones, missiles and atomic bombs. But no need to worry, as Albert Einstein told us—the war after the next one will be fought with sticks and stones. And we might add, that if we don't thin out our populations voluntarily, that next war will do it for us. But do we really want another "war to end all wars?" We had two in the last century and we still have some world leaders rattling their atomic sabers.

We see today, the combination of:

- Too many people for a family or nation to support,
- Too few people educated to the level necessary in today's technological society,
- Too many migrants fleeing their environs from poverty and war,
- Too many migrant freeing to opportunity,
- Empathy for the migrants who didn't choose their birth situations,
- Reduction of empathy as an excess of migrants disrupt the accepting societies (economic costs, religious and social class differences,--and often: job losses of the native born and the possibility of increased criminality)

Many believe that the increase in the dissatisfied among us should be stopped at the source, preventing their births rather than asking other countries to welcome them after they are grown. Poland is a case in point. With more than 38 million people, who are aging, they need more people to pay for the increasing number of retirees. But with a native-born population of 97%, they certainly don't want non-Polish immigrants—although over 1.2 million Poles have left their country for greener employment pastures. So they closed their borders to people who want in, but open them for people who want out. Men retire at 65 so need 12 years of pension. Women retire at 60 so need 20 years of pension.

How should they solve their problems? Raise retirement ages? No! Bring in immigrant workers? No! Encourage more births? Yes! They have done this by giving $135 per child from the second child (for the first child for poor mothers), and a minimum retirement for mothers of four. Thank you Poland, for your efforts to increase climate change.

In the Southern Hemisphere, Sub-Saharan Africa has reduced birthrates from 6.7 per woman in 1985 to 4.8 today—but that is still more than the world or the family needs today. Somalia at 6.2 and Mali at 6.0 are a shade higher than Mauritius at 1.4 and South Africa at 2.4. But don't worry, Europe will take the excess!

Whoops! Many in Europe now oppose taking in immigrants. Poland and Hungary have erected walls. A recent poll in 2018, found that majorities in all seven polled countries were opposed to accepting more migrants: Germany (72%), Denmark (65%), Finland (64%), Sweden (60%), United Kingdom (58%), France (58%) and Norway (52%). So empathy is waning. Will the overpopulated countries attempt to curb births? Will the world assist them? Or will our age-old traditions continue to bless parenthood while the increased population curses the planet?

OUR TRADITIONS ARE THE HURDLES IMPEDING OUR PROGRESS

When we talk about overcoming traditions, it is extremely difficult. Whether you are having to take public transportation rather than drive your car, stop burning wood in your fireplace, using plastic Christmas trees instead of the carbon-catching millions of fir trees we have traditionally killed every winter to celebrate the birth of Light and the advent of Armageddon. Or, what about refraining from using your home electrical system, when the electricity comes from burning fossil fuels--it is disconcerting, if not downright troublesome. But these nuisances are minuscule when we compare them with reducing population--not having a child that you want. This can be a major impediment to reversing climate change--but it is THE major one! It is the elephant in the room that nobody wants to see!

Great thinkers have suggested utopias that would challenge our lethargy. Rousseau would have us return to the mythical days of the noble savages—to equality. Plato gave us the blueprint for the ideal method of being governed—but we continually reject the ideal. History is clear that to thin out our population we need a great war and a great warrior—a Caesar, a Tamerlane, a Napoleon, or a Tojo. Swords and spears, or bullets and bombs, are the guillotines of our hopes and prayers.

Will collective intelligence ever override the flow of fear and the whimper of hope that have pulled our human race to the brink of Niagara?

CAN WE SLAY THE TYRANTISAURUS OF TRADITION—AND SAVE OURSELVES?

If we encourage or require people to reduce their family size, we run afoul of many religions and our species-long requirement for preservation by reproduction. Tribes or countries with more young men become formidable adversaries. Warriors have always been a necessity. As trade, and lots of lots of manufacturing, became the marks of a successful country, consumers were needed. In the more primitive areas of our world, and sometimes in the developed world, the man or woman with many children could point to his or her fecundity as a mark of their superiority.

China's "one child" policy is continually bashed for three reasons:

1. It impeded people's freedom,
2. Abortions of female fetuses has resulted in 30 million more males, and,
3. More workers are needed to support China's greying population.

These are true, but they don't tell the whole story. The 400 million fewer children born allowed for the elimination of poverty in the country, better education for all, the funding of economic infrastructure, the significant increase in living standards, and the number of millionaires and billionaires.

The World Bank set the international poverty line at $1.90 per day in 2015, but each country sets its own standards for poverty. In the U.S. it is $32 a day for a single person under 65 and $67 a day for a family of four. The CIA World Factbook for 2018 lists: China with 2.7% living in poverty, the U.S. with 15.1%, the UK with 15%, Haiti with 59%, Zimbabwe 72.3%, and war-torn Syria with 82.5% of its population in poverty.

On the other end of the economic scale, China is second to the U.S. in the number of billionaires—285 to 705. (Compare to Germany with 146, Russia 102, and UK with 97.) Also, of October 2019, there were more Chinese than Americans in the world's richest 10%. The average (mean) incomes (total earnings divided by the number of income earners) are deceptive because the millionaire and billionaire incomes raise the average. A more accurate picture would be seen by looking at the median income—the income of the earner at the exact middle of all earners.

Per capita incomes	1980	2018	% Increase
United States	$48,400	$62,800	23%
United Kingdom	$39,400	$43,400	9%
China	$4,500	$9,770	117%
World	$9,500	$11,300	16%

The obvious point is—if a rapid increase of income, and what it can do for increasing one's ability to acquire higher education and/or travel extensively, increases one's freedom, reducing population is a very positive factor in freedom. With the average cost of raising a child to age 21 in the United Kingdom of 273,000 British pounds ($358,000) and $233,000 to raise a child in the U.S.to age 18, plus expenses for college for the next few years –you can see the financial freedom advantages to having fewer children.

IT IMPEDED PEOPLE'S FREEDOM

According to the World Bank, more than 850 million Chinese people have been lifted out of extreme poverty. We might assume that poverty somewhat affects peoples' freedom! Am I wrong, here? China's poverty rate fell from 88 percent of its population in 1981 to 0.7 percent in 2015.

Then there is their progress in developing university educational opportunities. In 2002, there were about 2000 higher education institutions in the People's Republic of China. Today there are 3,000 and three are rated in the top 100 in the world. More than 28 million students are currently studying in them, this is the same number as in the U.S. Additionally, last year 662,000 Chinese students left China to study at overseas universities. This was about 70,000 more than the year before. Most return home with new knowledge and ideas.

China is doing quite well in producing STEM (science, technology, engineering, mathematics) graduates. Only Russia and Iran produce more technical graduates as a percentage of their populations—and they were both well ahead of China in 1980, when the "one child" policy was implemented.

STEM graduates

Country in millions	Population in millions	STEM graduates per million	% of pop.
China	1,433	4,700	3.2
India	1,56	2,600	1.9
US	330	568	1.7
Russia	146	561	3.8
Iran	83	335	4.0
Indonesia	270	206	0.7
Japan	126	195	1.5

Those of us who regularly attend scientific conferences can attest to the unbelievable advancement of Chinese science. When Chinese scientists presented their work from about 1990 to 2000, we smiled. They were discovering things with the same instruments that we in the West had discovered in the 1950s. But by 2010 they were state of the art. Their scientific instruments and their knowledge of their scientific fields had leap-frogged over the decades. The increased money available, since they didn't have to educate and care for 400 million children, became available to send their students to the best universities in the world and to finance their rapid economic development.

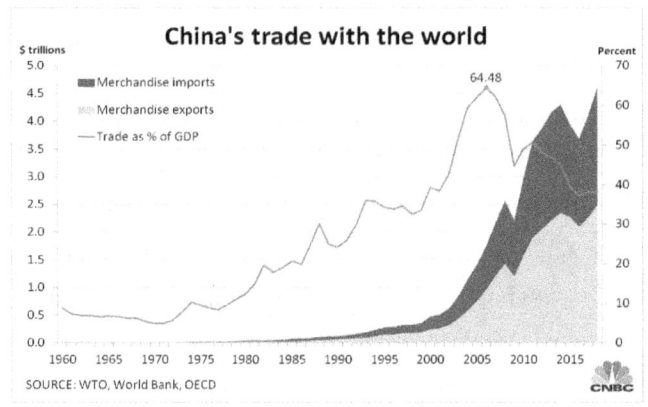

Does this sound like the Chinese people's freedom was impeded a great deal because some of them could not have more than one baby?

ABORTIONS OF FEMALE FETUSES HAS RESULTED IN 30 MILLION MORE MALES

This is true, but it is a result of an antiquated family tradition—not of the one child policy. Males were supposed to be better able to support their aging parents—but that was before women were allowed to attend the universities and enter the workforce in highly paid jobs. The long-held idea that women should be barefoot and pregnant in the kitchen has been submerged with the blessings of contraception and safe abortions that have allowed women the same opportunities as men.

In the U.S. 56% of university students are female. In China it is 52.5%. It is also the majority in the UK. So, if taking care of aging parents is important, women will be better able to do it.

MORE WORKERS ARE NEEDED TO SUPPORT CHINA'S GREYING POPULATION.

This is a concern in many countries. Short-sighted vote-hungry politicians have assumed that there will always be 5 or 6 workers paying into their inadequate pension funds to pay for the retirees who were never required to contribute enough to pay for their pensions.

If we continue to increase the population, with 5 to 7 new workers to pay for the older workers, we will need geometrically more workers every generation. So if we need five more workers now to support each retiree, in 20 to 40 years we will need 25, Then 40 more years 125 workers to support the 25 of the last generation. All this while the number of employees needed is reducing because of robotics, computerization, 3D printing, and artificial intelligence.

If we calculate the number of people needed to support every worker in retirement, and if only half of today's population of 7,500,000,000 works and we need five workers to support each retiree, in forty years we will need 18.5 billion workers. Then forty years later we will need 90 billion workers. It wouldn't be too long before we would need a population of a trillion people. But that will never happen because floods, famines and hurricanes will wipe out a large number of us. Our politicians seem to keep getting us deeper and deeper into the quicksand of our own genocide. But it really doesn't matter as long as they keep getting elected. In fact, if we elect the appropriate people, they will assure us that climate change doesn't exist and that any abortion is terribly wrong. Certainly, the world needs more children—especially those who are not wanted.

RETIREMENT AGES

American retirement age has increased only two years in the last 80. In the US when Social Security was enacted, the retirement age was 65 and the average lifespan was 64. We have recently raised the retirement age to 67, for those born since 1960, but our lifespans are in the early 80s—and increasing.

In the U.S., our retirement contributions are generally used up by our early 70s. The government must then make up for our lack of adequate contributions for 5 to 10 more years of our retirement.

As I remember, one of those messages carved in stone on Mount Sinai was that we should be able to retire at age 65. Most blasphemous countries allow it to be between 55 and 60. I hope there's enough oil under their workplaces to support 30 years of retirement!

China recently increased the number of children allowed per family to two. There were several reasons for this. One of which was to provide a workforce to support the aging population.

Lifespans in China have increased from 35 years in 1948 to 66 years in 1976 to 76 years today. Retirement age is between 50 and 55 for women and 6o for men. How much will today's young workers need to contribute for their extra 15 to 20 years of retirement?

The retirement age in China currently is 60 for men and 55 for female civil servants and 50 for female workers. By 2038 there will be an equal retirement age for women and men set at 67. (Women's retirement age will reach 65 in 2030 and 67 in 2038).

Tradition continually blocks our thinking about issues. For China, rather than having more children, they might raise the age of retirement to 68 or 70 for both men and women. Of course, the people will object and possibly rebel. Look at what happened in Russia and France in 2019 when their presidents attempted to tackle tradition and inch closer to a realistic pension plan. Demonstrations and riots erupted. So don't mess with traditions—no matter how antiquated and harmful to society they are. Astute politicians will always give the electorate what they want. Let their children pay for it in taxes or in a national bankruptcy.

ENOUGH OF CHINA—HOW ABOUT THE REST OF US?

With Pope Francis condemning atomic war, but encouraging more children to be born, is he seeing the whole picture? Do ExxonMobil and Koch Industries, going after profits today, realize that their future consumers will be significantly reduced with the growing specter of mass annihilation? Do the Mormons, seeking to free the infinite number of souls that were created when God started us on our fateful path, understand that the present surge of souls will be reduced to a trickle? Reducing the number born now will result in more available souls to save than would be available if we experience a catastrophic series of population reducing calamities--like mass famines and gigantic storms.

A GLANCE AT PEOPLE AND POLLUTION

The most emissions from fossil fuels come from China and the United States. In terms of CO_2 emissions *per capita* per year, China is ranked only 47th, at 7.5 metric tons per capita. The US is ranked 11th at 16.5 tons per capita. India is the third highest country in terms of absolute emissions, but only 158th in terms of per capita output with 1.7 metric tons per capita.

Australia has an average per capita footprint of 17 tons, and Canada has 15.6 tons per capita. So reducing population in the U.S., Canada or Australia by one person will be about the same as reducing 150 to 200 people in Somalia or Eritrea in terms of fossil fuel use!

Wait a minute! In much of southern Africa, especially east Africa, there are some big problems. CO_2 absorbing forests are being reduced significantly. This is done for firewood and charcoal production. So, Africa is a problem too.

The United Nations' IPCC estimates that about 15% of carbon dioxide is emitted from wood-burning for cooking fires in Africa. There are about 2.1 billion people in Africa living below the poverty line.

In countries in East Africa, such as in Somalia, Zambia, and Madagascar, charcoal is produced for sale to other African countries for cooking, to Arab countries for hookka smoking, and world-wide for barbeque cooking. This charcoal production is usually done illegally on government lands—and is illegal according to the United Nations. The trees that are chopped down are not replaced. Obviously then, the wood is burned—releasing its carbon onto the atmosphere and carbon-capturing trees are lost in the process.

In the last six years in Somalia, 8.2 million trees have been removed. In Uganda the forest cover has been reduced in the last 15 years from 24% to 9%. So Africa's contribution to greenhouse gas production is not reflected in the charts we see of the greenhouse gases that are produced from burning fossil fuels—like coal, oil, gasoline, other gases and from permafrost thawing.

Somalia makes about half of the African profits from total charcoal sales of $360 million a year. The al Qaeda linked al Shabab takes about 10% of this profit as protection money, which it uses to fund its terrorist activities. So we have another unexpected villain on our highway to survival!

Across Africa the charcoal trade is destroying the forest cover which has been absorbing the CO_2 emissions from cooking fires and from industry. The European Space Agency has found that biomass (ie. wood, manure) burning is responsible for about 30% of climate changing greenhouse gases. Congo has the second largest forest in the world—after the Amazon. The increasing population needs more jobs and more cooking charcoal—so the forest and the world suffer.

Truck full of charcoal in Somalia

You can imagine that burning over a million trees a year is adding to the greenhouse effect caused by the carbon dioxide released. So rich and poor people are contributing to the warming--yes, the rich are worse, but we are all a part of the problem.

We know that there is a strong relationship between income and per capita fossil fuel CO_2 emissions. But Europe is doing a far better job than other major polluting countries. The global average of carbon dioxide emissions is about 4.8 tons per person. Some European countries have emissions not far from the global average: Portugal is about 5.3 tons and France and the UK are just a bit higher than Portugal—because they are producing much of their energy from renewable and nuclear sources. But China's CO_2 emissions per capita have more than tripled in the past 15 years.

You are probably already protesting against removing many of the benefits that our economic system and our technological pampering has given us--undreamed of comforts and conveniences. We no longer have to walk great distances to talk to a friend. We don't have to send smoke signals either. We can e-mail, Skype, Facetime, Facebook, WhatsApp or even drive to see each other. We don't have to work 10 or 12 hours a day, 6 or 7 days a week, to make a living. There are more ways to kill a night than just playing cards. We had radio, then television, the Internet—and now video games. Life keeps getting easier, with more free time and more enjoyable ways to spend it. How come? More fossil fuel is available for our transportation needs. There is more electrical power for our air conditioning, heating, TVs, and for research to make life even easier.

So, our long-held traditions, and even our recently acquired traditions, must be adjusted as climate change heats our air, increases the intensity of our storms, and makes forest fires more likely and more damaging.

We must expect more atmospheric problems to darken our days—both heat and cold as well as wet and dry. Our taxes will rise.

INCREASED TAXES OR NATIONAL DEBT

Our national debts will increase—if we can still find people to lend to us! We may even find it necessary to change our economic system. Governments rely on two or three sources for the money that fuels them.

➢ Immediate Taxes (sales, income, property, etc.)

➢ Delayed Taxes (borrowing, and printing currency—interest or devaluation are immediate, loan principle due later)

➢ Government ownership of part or all of some industries. (Profits are used to reduce taxes, rather than to enrich capitalists.)

American politicians call socialism (government ownership of all or part of the industries) totally unacceptable. The U.S. relies on the first two options to finance itself, although it does own the Postal System, the Tennessee Valley Authority, mortgage and loan companies (Freddie Mac, Fannie May) and a number of other businesses. So the United States is partially socialistic. Not as much as most modern countries, which may be one of the reasons that the U.S. is only 18th on the UN international happiness scale. (For more on this read: "Make America Great Again—Like Norway.")

Except for Bernie Sanders, Americans decry socialism. Few see that their sacred Social Security System is communistic ("as Karl Marx wrote, "From each according to his ability to each according to his needs."). Medicaid is equally communistic, being based on need. Medicare is more socialistic since it only covers those who paid in. (Lenin said that "Socialism is from each according to his ability, to each according to his work.") Even the government-paid educational systems, which are becoming more common around the world, can be considered to be communistic since they are available to all for a certain number of years.

So our anti-communist and anti-socialist traditions are overlooked when something, we see as good, sneaks into our capitalist global view. The U.S. didn't have Social Security until the mid-30s. Thirty years later President Lyndon Johnson began the enactment of laws that eventually led to Medicaid and Medicare—and more traditions were absorbed into the abyss of tradition.

What could be next?—Eu-genics (reducing potential genetic or epigenetic problems, such as genes related to violence, psychosis, low intelligence, etc.), eu-parenting (parent licensing—to ascertain potential parent's abilities and aptitudes for financial and psychological caretaking), required sterilization, voluntary sterilization, taxing children, etc. Or should we allow, or encourage, the unrestricted increase of population.

The reality of unrestricted family size will certainly increase ecological problems such as: decrease of natural resources, decreasing fresh water available, increasing air and water pollution, increased greenhouse gases, increasing northward and westward migration, with the strong possibility of more wars (water-wars and wars for more territory), and more terrorism.

There are too many people in the world. Some of them are very good for the world as scientists, some legislators, creative entrepreneurs, artists, etc. Some are very bad for the world, like: warlords, terrorists, criminals, and abusers of different sorts. we might even add here those who cannot contribute to the society because of inherited inabilities.

Of course, if we begin to eliminate potential citizens, we run the risk of criticism from religions and other groups. For example, if we were to attempt to instigate a family-planning program in Mali, Nicaragua, or India, we would probably be accused of genocide. But then, if we don't thin out the population, we are all potential victims of genocide. So, do we want our greenhouse gases to kill or inconvenience most of the population of the world, or do we aid in lowering the fertility rate in some areas while we improve their educational opportunities and their chances for happiness. The United Nations happiness scale does not list those countries with high fertility rates in the same high categories as those with lower fertility rates.

When we look at some of the high fertility rate countries, we often see children being sold into slavery or released into the overpopulated cities without parents. CNN recently aired a program, originating in Africa, where boys as young as four had been given to a supposedly religious man who ran schools. The boys were released every morning with buckets to beg for money or hopefully they would find jobs. They were given quotas of money they had to bring back to the adults. They slept in the open-air in slums. Is this what you would want for your children?

When we look at eugenics, people will say that that is what Hitler did. One should not criticize an idea because of the person who advocated it, rather than for the idea being expressed, this is called a logical fallacy. In fact, it is called the *ad hominem* fallacy. The fact is that Hitler loved his mother intensely. He said she was the most important person in his life. Should we therefore criticize all people who love their mothers? In the United States a number of years ago, eugenics was used to stop the reproduction of some African-Americans.

Hitler's plan was to eliminate those who he thought were inferior: the Jews, the Slavs, homosexuals, and the physically or mentally handicapped. But he also had a plan to increase the number of people in the higher "master race." So he encouraged the high level men to father with a high level women.

WHAT ARE SOME OPTIONS TO REDUCE POPULATION?

We will look at some options for reducing population—but it is not enough to say that we must do something, we must look deeper at the hows and the whys. For example, it is not enough to tell Poland that they must immediately stop burning coal. 80% of its electricity is generated from the work of the 100,000 coal miners. The economics of Poland is a major concern for them. The survival of the planet's population is a concern for the rest of us. It is the narrowly viewed NOW versus the future of humanity. How do we solve the problem?

In the concern for overpopulation, we have the same "now verses the future" problem. We will suggest some guidelines for the population of the future, but people won't like the possibilities. They flaunt tradition! But they need to be outlined if we are going to attempt to survive—and survive in a cooperative and more peaceful world.

So here goes!—Some ideas for reducing and improving the society that is threatening their home!

VOLUNTARY

These options may need financial assistance from richer countries to poorer countries.

➤ Abortion on demand.

➤ Euthanasia on demand. This could include not only sick people, but others who wish to die. There are about 800,000 suicides in the world annually, 47,000 in the U.S.

➤ Contraceptives on demand.

➤ Sterilizations on demand.

➤ Enticement to voluntary sterilization by monetary awards from governments or private sources.

MANDATORY AND SEVERE

One option is to do nothing now, but to let Nature takes its course as the warming climate increases violent storms, larger forest fires, and more extensive famines—and possibly more wars and terrorism as various physical and social stresses lead to violence. More migration is already happening. Water wars and the closing of borders to immigrants are strong possibilities—both have happened in the past.

We are all going to die—that is determined when we are born. Is it imperative to do all things possible to protect and extend every life? Should mass shooters, when found guilty, languish in taxpayer paid prisons while they contribute to global warming after causing the deaths of productive and innocent people? Should Hitler or Attila or John Wilkes Booth have been drowned at birth? Should there be any criteria to live freely? We now have severe penalties for murderers—even death in many countries!

Are all lives equal? Are all lives equally valuable—even when they are anti-social? Even though they do not contribute to the society? Even if they are terminally ill? If so, we might consider some other options, even if they run counter to UN and EU rights.

➤ One option would be to have national or international lotteries that would allow the lucky winners to have a child. The recent United Nations and European Union protocols for treating everyone equally might approve of this—except that those who didn't win, were not treated equally.

➤ China's recent "one child policy" treated people equally, but restricted the liberty of those who wanted more children. The radical reduction in family size –from a fertility rate of 3.81 in 1975 to 1.7 today—will not be realized as a downturn in their population until about 2050. The 70 year lag, from the introduction of the program until a population reduction is realized, is too long a period to have the immediate effect we need today.

➤ Increased capital punishment with speedier appeals and executions—possibly increasing capital crimes to: rape, child molestation, illegal drug sellers, and maybe even tax evaders and burglars!

➤ People who choose to use dangerous drugs, then overdose, could be left to die. Many are not contributing to the society—and they bring in more criminal suppliers.

➤ As the importance of genetics became known, "eugenics" has been considered and used. The equalitarian emphasis of today's politics makes it a long-shot option. But it will be discussed below.

➤ Eu-parenting, while never used, has been suggested with varying parental qualities and abilities being the necessities for parent licensing. The equalitarian bent of democratic thinking makes this option another long-shot. While legally all children belong to the state, it nearly always lets the natural or adoptive parents raise them—even when the children are abused or neglected. It will also be discussed below.

Attempts to reduce populations in India, Africa, Brazil or Boston will elicit cries of "genocide," while producing more polluters is somehow praiseworthy! Just look at the religious accolades afforded to the Duggar family with their 19 children. A reality TV show contract and lots of positive publicity was their reward. The last I heard there were nine grandchildren for this ever-expanding family. But if we only look a little deeper, we see that their neighbors had to pay taxes to put these children through school—about $3,600,000. Then there is the carbon footprint, of every child, of 20 metric tons of carbon dioxide per year. That is about 400 metric tons per year for the family, and if each lives to be about 80 years old, it will be about 32,000 metric tons of carbon dioxide for each person—or about 640,000 metric tons during the lives of the immediate family. So the Duggar family, not counting the grandchildren, has a carbon footprint equivalent to 87 American cars each driven 12,000 miles per year. So, "yea!" for the family that was fruitful and multiplied! But then there is the carbon footprint of each child and their children, and their children—if the world survives!

These good Baptists followed their holy book—where it tells us in Genesis 1:28 to "... Be fruitful and multiply." But they might have read the whole verse:

"And God blessed them, and God said unto them, Be fruitful, and multiply, and replenish the earth, and subdue it: and have dominion over the fish of the sea, and over the fowl of the air, and over every living thing that moveth upon the earth."

It seems that the earth is more "replenished" than it has ever been. And certainly, the descendants of Adam and Eve have not subdued it. In fact, the earth now seems to be subduing those descendants! And what about all of us living things that moveth upon the earth? We have done a terrible job of dominating us and our world!

TOO MANY PEOPLE USING TOO MUCH FOSSIL FUEL!

There are too many people in the world. Some of them are very good for the world as scientists, effective legislators, creative entrepreneurs, some artists, etc. Some are very bad for the world, like: warlords, terrorists, criminals, and abusers of different sorts. We might even add here, those who cannot contribute to the society because of inherited inabilities.

GENOCIDE

Of course, if we begin to eliminate potential citizens, we run the risk of criticism from religions and other groups. For example, if we were to attempt to instigate a family-planning program in Mali, Nicaragua, or India, we would probably be accused of genocide. But then, if we don't thin out our population, we are all potential victims of genocide. So, do we want our greenhouse gases to kill or inconvenience most of the population of the world or do we aid in lowering the fertility rate in some areas while we improve their educational opportunities and their chances for happiness. The United Nations happiness scale does not list any of those countries with high fertility rates in the same high categories as those with lower fertility rates.

When we look at some of the high fertility rate countries, we often see children being sold into slavery or released into the overpopulated cities without parents. CNN recently aired a program, originating in Africa, where boys as young as four have been given to supposedly religious man who ran schools. The boys were released every morning with buckets to beg or hopefully to find jobs. They were given quotas of money they had to bring back to the adults. They slept in the open-air in slums. Is this what you would want for your children?

Generally, the more children a family has the lower their happiness level. (For those interested in seeing more details on this, we suggest reading "**A Global Perspective on Happiness and Fertility" by Rachel MaRgolis and Mikko MyRskylä at:**

https://www.ncbi.nlm.nih.gov/pmc/articles/PMC3345518/

THE BIG QUESTIONS

The first question is—Shall we attempt to limit population?

The second is--should we try to control the types of people, since modern life seems to need more intelligent and more loving people. Math and science aptitudes and training, not manual labor are needed—and even more important, people who are loving and not intent on shooting, raping and robbing us. How can we do these things? Do we want to?

If we want to raise the intelligence level of the population, and possibly change a tendency for other elements of personality—like violence, lack of impulse control, and sexuality—we have some knowledge about how to do this. For this we must look at eugenics and epigenetics. For developing a well-balanced person with the ability to love, parenting is essential—and eugenics may also play a role.

INFANTICIDE

We could just kill unwanted babies. But this idea is generally frowned on in today's more advanced cultures. However, it has been practiced since prehistoric times. Many Neolithic sites have been unearthed confirming this practice. It is clear that family sizes had to be controlled because there was not enough food for the family or tribe. In many later cultures, child sacrifice to the gods became common. It has been found throughout the Middle Ages, and we see it today in many societies, including our own. How often have you heard of a young woman leaving her newborn in a dumpster?

We know that it was quite common in ancient Greece and Rome—in fact the mythological founders of Rome, Romulus and Remus, had been thrown in the Tiber River before being rescued and raised by a wolf.

Primitive tribes and cultures, as well as the destitute or unwilling today, have unburdened themselves of surplus infants. While the Abrahamic religions of Judaism. Christianity and Islam have generally opposed infanticide, Christians have often opted for a more comfortable life here and now, rather than waiting for the hereafter with a large brood of starving children huddled in cramped corners. 19th century England records many illegal infanticides and the hanging of many murderous mothers.

EUGENICS

Modern eugenic ideas have been around as long as genetics has been studied. Sir Francis Galton, a major mid-19th Century scientific genius, coined the term "eugenics." He was a highly regarded scientist and mathematician. His forays into science and his extensive traveling opened many doors. He invented the concept of correlation as well as coining the word "eugenics" and the term "nature versus nurture." He pioneered the field of behavioral genetics with his "twin" studies-- researching whether identical twins raised in different environments would be different and whether fraternal twins raised in the same environment would be similar. His observations led him to believe in both eugenics and in equality of opportunity-- by increasing inheritance taxes to form a tax base for supporting genetically gifted poorer people to be able to have more superior children.

As previously mentioned, people will say that eugenics is a bad idea because Hitler advocated eugenics. But, one should not criticize an idea because of the person who advocated it, rather than for the idea being expressed.

The fact is that Hitler's ideas followed those of American and German scientists. California led the way in sterilizing unfit people in the early 1900s. In the 1930s Hitler continued with such sterilizations, then with gas chambers. (That was certainly extreme!) He also required people who planned to marry to undergo testing to uncover any tendency to hereditary diseases.

Hitler's idea was to eliminate: the Jews, who were religiously and racially inferior, the Slavs who were racially inferior. He also wanted to get rid of the homosexuals and physically and mentally inferior people, who were usually institutionalized in state or private facilities—because they were not normal and stood in the way of his development of his "master race" development plans.

Eugenics was also supported by African-American intellectuals such as W. E. B. Du Bois and many academics at the traditionally black colleges: Tuskegee University, Howard University, and Hampton University. They believed that the best blacks were as good as the best whites and that "The

Talented Tenth" of all races should mix. Du Bois believed "only fit blacks should procreate to eradicate the race's heritage of moral iniquity."

In Michigan a compulsory sterilization bill was introduced in 1897, but was not passed. In 1905 Pennsylvania passed a sterilization bill, but it was vetoed by the governor. Two years later Indiana passed such a eugenic law. Several states quickly followed. The U.S. Supreme Court, in 1927, allowed for sterilization for some patients in a home for the mentally retarded in Virginia. Fifteen years later it disallowed the sterilization of prisoners. From 1910 and for 50 years there were 60,000 U.S. sterilizations—20,000 in California. North Carolina allowed sterilization of people with an IQ below 70—the bottom 3% of the intellectual population.

As we all know, purebred dogs, thoroughbred horses and every type of domesticated animal have been genetically improved. But faulty genes can also be passed on.

EU-PARENTING AND PARENT LICENSING

Looking deeper at the overpopulation, we should see that it is not enough to reduce the total population, if we want a peaceful, cooperative, contended, happy and productive world, we must attempt to reduce genetic diseases, reduce negative epigenetic changes (environmental stresses that may affect how genes function), and do what we can to insure that children are raised in a loving and emotionally nourishing environment.

There is a great deal of evidence that genetic tendencies, aroused or quieted by epigenetic and environmental factors are significantly related to both childhood and adult tendencies to abuse—from bullying to terrorism. So if we are to look at controlling the quantity of population, we should also look at improving the quality of the population by upgrading the quality of parenting.

There is no situation as pleasant and exciting as the frivolity that usually goes with the release of sperm that may impregnate an ovum and begin the process that eventually leads to birth, then death. But the simplicity of the start of impregnation does not signal the complicated consequences of the birth, education, and development of the child and adolescent that resulted from that moment of pleasure. So simple to start a life-- so difficult to develop a loving, healthy and educated young adult.

In order for the embryo and fetus to develop into a healthy baby requires the proper nutrition of the mother, competent medical attention, and a pregnancy which is as stress-free as is possible. We have known for many years that genetics are important, if not essential, for a healthy baby. For the last 30 years we have become aware that epigenetics (the science of environmental effects that can change the functions of the genes, making them active or inactive.

We now know that certain experiences of parents or other ancestors can be passed on to a child. Alcoholism, drug use or abuse, starvation or overeating, and to a large degree--stresses of various sorts, can inactivate genes that may be essential in the ability of the child to live fully. As safe as you may think life is in the placenta, research shows that stresses undergone by the mother can seriously affect the genes of the developing embryo or fetus. Stresses throughout life, especially early in life, can have significant effects on the development of a child and adolescent. These may be registered as epigenetic changes on the genes or as conscious or unconscious scars on the psyche.

Then there are the obvious needs of a child: nutrition, disease prevention, emotional warmth and love, education and a number of other factors that can positively or negatively affect the child or adolescent.

Raising a child is probably the most important job in the world. It requires a significant knowledge of nutrition, medicine, psychology, and educational attainment-- along with the relatively rare ability to love. We could also say that a certain amount of money will be needed to assure that the child has its physical needs met.

Barbers and cosmetologists, doctors and nurses, teachers and drivers-- all need licenses. They also all need training. What kind of training does a parent need? As indicated above, it should be extensive. Plus, we would need to be certain that the parents had the ability to love the child.

While a basic knowledge of nutrition and health may be easily obtained, understanding the psychological needs of the child is extremely complicated. So let us look for a few minutes at some of the needs of a child as it grows. We can see here why it would be so difficult to develop a license for parents. But we can also see why prospective parents should have such basic knowledges. If we were to require a knowledge of child psychology in order to have a child, probably many people would opt out-- and solve our population problem!

We will look for a few moments at what a few of the major world authorities on children and adults have to say. First we will summarize some of the thoughts of psychologists and educators such as Erik Erikson and Robert Havighurst. Then we will see what Erik Fromm has to say about psychological needs and how the ability to love develops. We will glance at what Abraham Maslow has to say about how our motivations. Then we will look at how Piaget and Kohlberg find how values are developed.

EU-PARENTING

A major question is whether or not children should have parents who can take care of them physically, emotionally, and educationally. Traditionally we have given the rights to adults to have children-- and to educate them the way they wish. We see both rich and poor adults who are highly competent as parents, and we see both rich and poor adults who are ineffective and often, highly destructive to their children. Some even murder them. Many abuse them severely both mentally and physically.

There is probably no activity more pleasant for the adults than the action of attempting to have the sperm meet a friendly ovum. From, there on there may be joys or pains through the period of pregnancy to childbirth.

After the birth, there is no job that requires the knowledge and the abilities to perform them as much as does parenthood. To be effective, it takes an incredible amount of the ability to love. It takes knowledge of the physical body, how it grows, and the physical and emotional needs of the child through the various stages of life. It requires a great deal of time. Many parents rationalize that they give quality time to their children since they don't have a great deal of the quantity of time to spend with them daily. In truth, children need both quantity and quality of time from their parents.

LICENSING PARENTS

What you find out in the United Nations Declaration of Human Rights is that it gives adults the right to "start a family." But it doesn't give the potential children the right to effective loving parenting. In fact, no rights for children begin until they are born.

We can't know if a child would prefer not to be born if he inherited physical diseases like hemophilia (inability of blood to clot), Down syndrome (severe learning disability), cystic fibrosis, Tay Sacks disease, sickle cell anemia, or any of the other genetic physical problems. Mental disorders may also be passed on genetically or epigenetically, such as: autism, attention deficit hyperactivity disorder (ADHD), bipolar disorder, major depression and schizophrenia.

Until recently, when the Israeli Supreme Court stopped the practice, children were suing their parents for "wrongful birth" because they wished they had never been born.

WRONGFUL BIRTH

In some jurisdictions, the child, sometimes with his or her parents, can sue the doctors or the hospital for not discovering a birth defect. California, India, The Netherlands (and previously Israel), have allowed for "wrongful life" actions when children are born with disabilities—or have lived unhappy lives.

In 2019, a businessman in Mumbai, India sued his lawyer parents saying that he should not have to suffer through life because of society's problems just because his parents wanted a few moments of pleasure.

"Wrongful life" or "wrongful birth" are the legal terms most commonly used where a child or the child's legal guardian sues the parents, the doctors, or the medical personnel involved in a birth that the offspring believes to be not in his or her interest. It may be because of faulty genetic testing, examinations during pregnancy, or being brought into a world that was not comfortable.

Such legal actions have been used in Israel by a number of disabled people who felt that their lives were miserable because of their birth. Some sued their parents. Some sued the medical profession. Parents also have been involved as plaintiffs against doctors or hospitals because they were not notified of potential genetic problems.

The Supreme Court of Israel has now made it illegal to sue for wrongful birth. The Supreme Court of California, however, has allowed it. In the 1982 case of Curlander v Bio-Science Laboratories, was a case in which the child was born with Tay-Sachs disease when the parents relied on the genetic testing of the laboratory and were not given the correct information, so did not proceed with amniocentesis. The Court's opinion included this paragraph:

"The reality of the 'wrongful-life' concept is that such a plaintiff both exists and suffers, due to the negligence of others. It is neither necessary, nor just, to retreat into meditation on the mysteries of life. We need not be concerned with the fact that had defendants not been negligent, the plaintiff might not have come into existence at all. The reality of genetic impairment is no longer a mystery. In addition, a reverent appreciation of life compels recognition that plaintiff, however impaired she may be, has come into existence as a living person with certain rights." (106 Cal Ap 3d 83)

The Curlander decision gives interested readers an extensive history of the cases in the U.S. that involve "wrongful life."

A similar case had a similar conclusion in New York, but it was overruled by the Supreme Court of New York. Many other states and countries have taken the same route, in disallowing wrongful birth actions. In Germany, the Federal Constitutional Court ruled that "the life of the disabled person is as valuable as a non-disabled person. because, human dignity is a basic concept in the German Constitution." But, the theoretical rationalization probably does not adequately comfort an unhappy, or miserable, living person. (As previously mentioned, our values can be based on self-centered assumptions, God-based assumptions, or society based assumptions. In this case, the complaining person was using self-centered assumptions, while the judges used a society-based, or possibly even a God-based, assumption. So we have the common conflict between value assumptions in our lives.)

(For those who would like to explore our values decision or the bases of our morality in depth, read "On Human Values," Book 4 of the free e-book series "And Gulliver Returns." The book is also available in print.)

In 2005, the Dutch Supreme Court upheld a lower court decision for a verdict for wrongful life.

Some courts have held that "nonexistent persons" do not have rights. This would of course indicate that life does not start until sometime after conception. In Israel, 600 cases for wrongful birth had been heard before the concept was made illegal.

In the Indian case the plaintiff's mother said that she "would destroy her son in court."

In the UK. a report by a cross-party committee found that almost one-in-five children under the age of 15 are growing up in a home that has "limited access to food ... due to lack of money or other resources." The 56-page report added. Yet, Britain is the world's fifth-richest country.

Then, we might look at the Preamble to the American Constitution, which sounds good but cannot be used in court. We will quote it again.

"We the people of the United States, in order to form a more perfect union, establish justice, insure domestic tranquility, provide for the common defense, promote the general welfare, and secure the blessings of liberty to ourselves and our posterity, do ordain and establish this Constitution for the United States of America."

We therefore might ask:

➢   Is it "just" to have babies born to parents who don't want them?

➢   Is it "just" to have babies born to parents who smoke, knowing the harmful effects of passive smoke?

➢   Is it "just" to have children born to alcoholics or to addicts of other drugs?

➢   Is it "just" to have children born into poverty when they may be malnourished or deprived of an adequate education?

We can ask the same questions about whether an unwanted child, or a child without a maximum chance at being the best that he or she can be, promotes the general welfare.

Would the child have a happier and more productive life if he or she were not physically or mentally afflicted? Would the parents have a happier life raising a child without these genetic problems? Would society be better off if it did not have to spend money attempting to right the genetic wrongs?

WHAT ABILITIES DO EFFECTIVE PARENTS NEED?

It takes an incredible amount of ability to love. It takes knowledge of the physical and emotional needs of the child through the various stages of life. It requires a great deal of time. Many parents rationalize that they give quality time to the children since they don't have a great deal of the quantity of time to spend with them daily. In truth, children need both quantity and quality time from their parents.

Licensing parents to have children has been suggested by a number of public figures. Child psychologist, Dr. Jack Westman wrote a very interesting book on parent licensing. ("Licensing Parents" 1994) One of his considerations was that young people should not have children because they have not had enough experience with life to handle parenthood. They also usually did not have a sufficient amount of money to take care of the economic needs of the child.

Dr. Hugh LaFollette, a philosopher, has written that parents need to be licensed. He is currently the Cole Chair in Ethics at the University of South Florida. He teaches and writes in ethics, especially practical ethics. He is author of books on applied ethics, such as gun control, and he is Editor-in-Chief of the International Encyclopedia of Ethics. See his article in the Princeton University Press in 1980: http://www.hughlafollette.com/papers/licensing.parents.pdf

The free e-book series, "And Gulliver Returns" looks at a number of obstacles to licensing parents and also at a number of requirements that psychologists and educators have considered important for a growing child. http://andgulliverreturns.info/

If drivers, barbers and plumbers must be licensed, is raising a child as important as driving a car, getting a haircut, or changing a water pipe? We require licenses for the pediatricians who might treat the child for illnesses. We require child dentists to have licenses, so that they can work effectively with the tooth fairy.

My nephew, who is an incredibly dedicated high school English teacher, and his wife, a licensed clinical social worker, wanted to adopt a black child. The adoption process took months of vetting them by the state of Nevada and cost them over $20,000 to become parents of an unwanted child. The birth parents were teenage Las Vegas high school students. These students didn't need to pay a fee, be thoroughly investigated, or have a license. The lucky child has two incredibly loving parents who are raising him in an unbelievably enriched environment.

But, I understand that there are some children born into this world who are starving. Others are physically and mentally abused. Still others are sex slaves. How sad!

WHO IS MORE IMPORTANT, THE CHILD, THE PARENTS, OR THE SOCIETY?

The needs of society are changing very rapidly. Throughout most of our human history, the economic needs were for hunters, herders, and farmers. More children were often an advantage. As our economic society developed we needed more trades-people and manufacturers. Now machines can do much of our work. But the machines require electrical energy. This often pollutes when it is generated. But we don't need as many people. The number of unemployed people in the world of working age is over 170 million. The world's unemployment rate is just under 8%. So, do we really need this many people? Then, there are the homeless—over a half million in the U.S. and more than a quarter million in the UK. 18 million Indian children live on the streets. Homelessness is not a new phenomenon—when I was in Calcutta 55 years ago on a government assignment, I was told that 3,000 people died on the street every day. Wouldn't it be nice to have a society in which all, or most, people were living in their own homes, were well-fed, and were productive and happy?

If we are to attempt to guarantee every child a physically nourishing and loving environment we could probably solve the population problem immediately. The problem is that adults are guaranteed the right to have children no matter how harmful they might be to them. Probably most of us would agree that every child should be born into a family that is not impoverished and that is physically and emotionally nourishing.

The World Health Organization tells us that one person in four is undernourished and that 45% of all deaths to children under five (3.1 million children annually) are related to malnourishment. One in four children is stunted from malnutrition one in six children (100 million) is underweight.

One in five children in rich countries are born into poverty: 38% in Mexico, about 19% in the US and the UK, in Israel it is nearly 35%. Even rich Norway and Denmark are in the 9 to 10% range. Every country has children born into poverty. 25% of people in India are living below of poverty line of $1.90 income per day.

The hopeful, but uninformed, people among us assume that every child will be loved and cared for effectively. Naturally, every parent loves his child! But what is love?

LOVE

One of America's greatest social thinkers, Ashley Montagu, was asked to write the chapter on love for the Encyclopedia of Mental Health. Before he could write about love, he had to define it.

We use the word "love" in so many ways that its meaning is generally confused.

➢ "I love pizza."

➢ "I love Mickey Mouse."

➢ "God loves me."

➢ "I love my wife."

➢ "I love my children."

We see here several meanings of the word "love." Generally we use it to say, "I approve of." Montague's definition was quite the opposite. He saw love as being unselfish and intelligently informed. Here is his definition:

"Love is the communication to another person, of one's deep involvement in that person's welfare, of one's profound interest in him as a person, demonstrated by acts that support, stimulate and contribute to the realization of that person's potential and to the fulfillment of their personality."

Is the alcoholic parent capable of loving? More than 10% of American children live in households with at least one alcoholic parent. What about the drug addicted parent? 3% live in households with a parent who is drug addicted. What about the parent who smokes? What about the parent who has no knowledge of nutrition? What about the parent who does not understand the psychological stages that children will probably pass through? What about the parent who wants the child for what the child can do for them, rather than what they can do for the child?

WHAT ARE THE PSYCHOLOGICAL AND EMOTIONAL NEEDS

It is obvious that parents should have a thorough knowledge of nutrition and diet, a knowledge of communicable diseases and how to prevent them, a knowledge of the importance of physical fitness and safety, a knowledge of how to educate the child effectively, and a knowledge of the psychological and emotional needs of the child. And, at least as important, is the ability to use these knowledges with the unselfish ability to love—and sometimes, infinite patience.

Looking at all of these ideals, we might wonder if any adults are capable of being effective parents!! Oh well, "perfection" is seldom, if ever, achieved—but we can, at least, strive to be better. And, certainly, all children born into the world should be raised by loving parents. So whether our main goal is to reduce climate change or foster a more effective society—giving all babies a real chance for a happy and productive life should be high on the list of the intelligent citizens of the world.

Let us look for a few moments at the informed observations of some highly respected psychologists and educators: Erik Erikson, Robert Havighurst and Abraham Maslow. Both Eric Erickson and Robert Havighurst have spent considerable portions of their lives studying the needs of children and adolescents. You may be interested in reading their thoughts.

Havighurst looked at both the physical and mental tasks that we must accomplish at each age. Erikson looked at the deeper psychological needs we must master. And, Maslow looked at the physical, emotional and intellectual needs we must fulfil to become "truly human" people.

HAVIGHURST

Robert Havighurst emphasized that learning is essential and that it continues throughout the life span. Growth and development occurs in six stages. He called these "developmental tasks."

Developmental Tasks of Infancy and Early Childhood:

1. Learning to walk.

2. Learning to take solid foods

3. Learning to talk

4. Learning to control the elimination of body wastes

5. Learning sex differences and sexual modesty

6. Forming concepts and learning language to describe social and physical reality.

7. Getting ready to read

Middle Childhood:

1. Learning physical skills necessary for ordinary games.

2. Building wholesome attitudes toward oneself as a growing organism

3. Learning to get along with age-mates

4. Learning an appropriate masculine or feminine social role

5. Developing fundamental skills in reading, writing, and calculating

6. Developing concepts necessary for everyday living.

7. Developing conscience, morality, and a scale of values

8. Achieving personal independence

9. Developing attitudes toward social groups and institutions

ERIKSON

Erikson called the early years of life the sensory stage. During this time the infant is a passive receiver of messages bombarding its senses. It is at this time, while the infant is totally dependent on others, that the first crisis is met. The baby learns whether to "*trust or mistrust*" the environment. This stage occurs during the first year or year-and-a-half of life. With the pursuit of money, rather than effective child raising, so common at every class level and with the great number of one-parent families, infants may have little opportunity to successfully meet this stage.

Erikson believed that a second stage, called the muscular development stage was next. If the child learns to control its muscular development (such as crawling, walking, and its bladder and bowel functions) successfully. It begins to feel that it is able to control the environment in some way. Erikson called this autonomy. But if there is a failure to adequately master one's musculature the child will develop a feeling of shame and will doubt its ability to successfully confront the world. This crisis Erikson called "*autonomy vs. shame and doubt.* " This should occur between the ages one and three.

How well a child handles these tasks is a major determinant as to whether he or she will develop a good feeling of self esteem or have a significant inferiority complex. These first few years are absolutely critical. It is highly unlikely that these tasks can be successfully completed in a day-care center. It is a very strong argument for one of the parents to be with the child most of the time during the first four or five years. (Who said parenting was easy??)

The locomotor control stage is a third stage which Erikson sees for our early years. The child attempts to find its own way-- to assert its needs and gain its rewards. Another problem of this age is that the child is attracted to the parent of the opposite sex (in Freudian terms, the Oedipus or Electra complex) and is somewhat alienated by the parent of the same sex. If the child is able to successfully solve the problems according to the behaviors which society considers acceptable, the child can be said to have developed "initiative. "If not, the child develops a sense of guilt which may remain forever as a part of its psychological make-up. This is called the crisis of "*initiative vs. guilt.*" This would probably occur about age four to five. With so many absent parents and one parent families, the child may have a difficult time meeting this need. The pursuit of money by so many parents may leave the children without the opportunity to solve this "crisis."

MIDDLE CHILDHOOD

According to Havighurst, from ages 6 to 11 new tasks are required to be learned. The developing child needs to learn:

1.   The physical skills necessary to play ordinary games (catching, throwing, kicking, swimming, handling simple tools),

2.   To build wholesome attitudes toward oneself as a growing person,

3.   To get along with others of the same age,

4.   To perform the appropriate social roles to function in the society,

5.   To use the basic intellectual tools such as reading, writing, mathematics,

6.   To develop basic concepts necessary for everyday living, such as ideas about health, history, geography, time, space, goal setting,

7.   To hold a value system and a set of morals to guide behavior,

8.   To develop a sense of independence,

9.   To develop democratic attitudes toward society.

While the parents have primary responsibility for the early years of development, both the parents and the school must take responsibility for these middle years of childhood. Many adults have not mastered all of these developmental tasks themselves. There are adults who are not independent. There are adults who do not subscribe to the democratic ethic. There are adults who cannot read or write or who do not understand the basic concepts of history, geography, or health.

Erikson saw a latent stage in our development. During this stage the child needs to become competent in dealing with the world. Success in school or games might develop a feeling of competence in the child. But failure to meet this crisis would result in a feeling of <u>inferiority and failure</u>. This is called the *"industry vs. inferiority"* crisis, and is likely to occur between ages six and eleven. This is another important step in developing self-esteem and eliminating or reducing inferiority feelings in the child.

Upper and middle class families are likely to put their children into sports, such as Little League, into dance lessons or music classes, or into Scout activities. Those in the lower social classes don't always have these opportunities. Their world may be limited to school and the streets around home.

EARLY ADOLESCENCE

According to Havighurst, from age 12 the child must learn to become more independent and to take care of himself or herself. At this age it is important to get along with others of the same age while developing appropriate social roles (often denoted as masculine or feminine). The child should be becoming more independent of parents while developing a moral-ethical system. It is also important to develop appropriate and wholesome attitudes toward the social groups and the institutions that make up the society.

Erikson saw this period of <u>puberty and adolescence</u> as requiring that the individual confront the crisis of "*identity vs. role confusion*." It is essential to determine how one will feel about one's sexuality. It is also important to develop a code of values and to make some decisions relative to what occupations one might pursue. The child must develop the idea that he or she is a special person--a special person who is responsible for himself or herself.

Many youth, particularly boys, get their "identity" through painting graffiti on walls. Many young girls get their identity by having sexual relations and becoming teenage mothers. Neither of these types of behaviors can be said to be "appropriate" in terms of developing a suitable self-concept.

LATER ADOLESCENCE

At this time in a person's life, the peer group usually becomes more important. It is essential to develop more mature relationships with age mates of both sexes. Sexual attraction becomes intensely important. The development of adult sex roles as masculine or feminine--understanding the expected roles of our culture as well as the potential roles which society is opening up-- is often more difficult to achieve. The traditional success oriented masculine role of provider is easier for boys to achieve than it is for girls. Even today girls often have to struggle to break the traditional nurturing role of wife-mother in order to satisfy their power drives in other areas, such as law, medicine, or business. But now, of course, most countries have more female students than males in the universities.

The maturing adolescent, according to Havighurst, must come to grips with the facts that he or she:

1.   Possesses a body which must be cared for;

2.   Needs to develop the intellectual skills and concepts necessary for civic competence;

3.   Must soon become psychologically independent of parents;

4.   Must develop the knowledge and skills necessary for economic independence;

5.   Must select and prepare for an occupation;

6.   Should prepare for marriage and family life, prepare to live independently, or prepare for an alternative companionate life style.

7.   Should develop a socially acceptable philosophy of life (a set of ethical standards necessary to behave in a socially responsible manner).

The best thing you can do for your children is not a financial inheritance but rather good genes and a healthy early environment. Warren Buffet, one of the world's richest men implied something like this when he said "Leave children enough money so that they feel they can do anything, but not enough so they can do nothing."

Parents who agree on how to raise their children are more effective than those who do not agree. Less authoritarian upbringing seems best. (This doesn't mean letting them do what they want-- but rather not telling them everything to do.)

All loving parents want to give their children whatever physical and emotional ingredients are necessary to make that child the best that it can be. In the 18 or so years that the child is under the parents' custody, the parents will be determining the physical, intellectual and emotional structure of the child. Many thousands of inputs will determine the body and character of the future adult. But where can the parent look for guidance? The myriad of books often confuse the baffled parent even more.

Children today love luxury. They have bad manners, a contempt for authority, a disrespect for their elders, and they like to talk instead of work. They contradict their parents, chatter before company, gobble up the best at the table, and tyrannize over their teachers.
SOCRATES, 5TH CENTURY, B.C.

INTELLECTUAL DEVELOPMENT

Intellectual development can be affected by the genes a child inherits and by the nutrition received in the womb and during the first years after birth. Psychologists have estimated that 7 per cent of children are born sufficiently defective so that their learning ability is impaired.

Whatever an infant's potential at the time of birth, it can be aided or frustrated by the environment in which it lives. The critical period in an infant's intellectual development begins at the age of seven months. By the age of three years, the child has usually mastered the beginnings of language which will be used in conversation throughout life, the adaptation to the role in the family, and many of the adjustment patterns which will be used during its lifetime. If the child is significantly behind others of the same age in these skills, it may be difficult to catch up. By the age of 4 approximately 50 per cent of the individual's intellectual development has taken place.

By eight years of age, approximately 80 per cent of the intellectual development has occurred.

Reading is the fundamental skill necessary to intellectual development. If a parent wants the child to learn to read, the best thing is to hold that child on one's lap and read stories aloud--over and over again, if necessary. The printed page, a reassuring voice, a fascinating story, and the physical comfort all indicate to the child that reading is a great source of pleasure. Cuddling is almost as important as the story in developing this idea. Of course, you can always buy a smart phone and let it raise your kids!

The United States Air Force recently compiled a list of indicators which may help to identify potential academic failure. Over-indulgent parents lead the list. A child should not be given all that he or she desires. The lessons of discipline and the rewards of work must be learned. Parents who coerce the child into studying can develop resentment against both the parents and the joy of learning.

Another factor leading to academic failure is starting the child to school too early. Just because a child is six-years-old does not mean that it is time to be in the first grade. People mature at different rates. Early academic failures may never be overcome. Unhappily, many parents are ashamed if their children are not "in the proper grade." But it is what is best for the child that should be considered to be primary. Other factors identified by the Air Force which were related to academic problems were: speech disorders, alcoholic parents, and premature birth.

VALUE DEVELOPMENT

Value development, like other areas of our development, is learned best by being rewarded for proper behavior rather than being punished for improper behavior, although either can be effective. We learn our values better by imitating our parents than by being told what to do.

All parents should remember that some day their children will follow their example, rather than their advice.

In every area of life, we have developed value standards. How fast we drive, how much we pay for food, and whether we cheat on tests, are all values that we have learned. Many of these are the result of parental influence. If you wish your children to develop certain values, you will need to develop an atmosphere of both freedom and limitation. That may sound incongruous, but the limitations put on a child often allow more freedom by giving the child mental boundaries and security.

Television has a great impact on the values of most of the children who watch it. It teaches them to cope with frustration through violence, develops their taste in cereals, and determines their lists for Santa Claus. The average first grader has watched 5,000 hours of TV and the average high-school graduate has spent 11,000 hours in class but 19,000 hours watching television, during which time 200,000 violent acts and 40,000 murders have been witnessed. It might be assumed that many of the young adults' values have been infused by the "tube." Other countries do not allow the violence to be shown on television but then their constitutions do not allow the often harmful "freedom of speech" that American entertainment corporations enjoy. And, they don't have the number of mass shootings of today's American wild west.

Television viewing is being somewhat reduced as social media and gaming take up our recreational time. The average teen-age girl spends over 9 hours a week gaming, boys spend over 16 hours. The average person spends slightly over an hour a day on social media—up from twenty minutes seven years ago. We are certainly being entertained, but are we spending much time constructively developing ourselves or our society--or the children we are raising?

It appears that making money is far more important to America than raising non-violent highly valued children. Of course, the movie and television industries might not have enough imaginative minds to create programs like Madam Secretary or Mash. It doesn't take a great deal of imagination to write a script with a car chase or have twenty people cut up with a chain saw or shot with an assault weapon.

The Scientific Advisory Committee to the Surgeon General reported that there is a causative relationship between televised violence and later anti-social behavior in many cases. The committee said very young children cannot distinguish between fantasy and reality on TV; the children also see each incident in a story as a whole, unrelated to the total story (i.e., they don't realize that the robber was caught and imprisoned for his crime--the crime and the capture are often unrelated in the child's mind). The report found that children spend more time watching adult shows than children's programs. And, because television is "sanitized, " the children do not see all of the facts such as, the mutilated body of the victim of a crime or accident, or the sorrow of a family which has been broken by the murder of one of its members.

Television can increase the child's vocabulary in early years. However, children who continue to watch television constantly during the teen-age years have been found to be less bright than the occasional viewers.

MORALS AND VALUES

The leading theorists of the psychology of morals are probably the Swiss psychologist Jean Piaget and the Harvard psychologist Lawrence Kohlberg. Dr. Kohlberg has identified six levels of moral behavior.

The first two levels of learning how to behave in an ethical way are called "pre-moral" and are typical of children and juvenile delinquents. Stage one is the obedience of the child through the fear of punishment. Stage two is called reciprocity. The child will do something good if rewarded. The reward should be tangible, like candy, money, or praise.

The second two levels are called "conventional" morality. Kohlberg believes that most teenagers and adults work at this level most of the time. Stage three is the level in which people do good in order to be looked upon with the esteem of others. During adolescence, the esteem may come primarily from the peer group rather than the family. Stage four occurs when people's behavior and their ideas of right and wrong are developed; they believe that, in order for society or a group to function, one must obey authority, such as the law.

The last two levels of behavior are based on "principle. " Stage five is based on the people working within a framework of rules upon which they have mutually agreed. This happens when people believe in the Constitution because they feel that the ideas were developed to protect individual liberties and rights. Only about 1 adult in 4 works at this level. The sixth level deals with universal principles. These moral principles are considered to be applicable to all human beings and are so important that one would give up one's life for one's principles. Very few people work at this level. Perhaps Mahatma Gandhi or Martin Luther King would be recent examples of such principled people.

Parents often try to teach values by preaching, but this isn't usually too effective. The father who advises against smoking while opening his second pack of cigarettes is not likely to be believed. Parents who realize the importance of the values that they are demonstrating for their children often reevaluate them. Parents cannot help but teach values. They may teach drunkenness, speeding, violence, or they may teach honesty, loyalty, and justice. It is a very important undertaking, deserving of some deep and honest thought. But whoever said that raising children was easy?

As indicated earlier, I am against most youth sports which are organized by adults. When children and adolescents organize their own games they make certain that the rules are enforced. In basketball they may say "Call your own fouls." Playing touch football in the streets the teen-agers won't tolerate unfair play and will exclude those who don't play fair. These children are working at the fourth and fifth levels of moral development (the development of right and wrong and working together with mutually formulated behaviors). But when parents come into the picture and referees are hired to "find" the illegal behavior and to penalize the guilty culprits, the players are back to level one (fear of punishment).

(Please don't read the foregoing as an anti-sport statement but rather as a pro-child statement. As one who has taught physical education for 40 years, is a lifetime member of the American Football Coaches Association and has coached football for over 40 years, I am definitely for sport. But not for the professionalization or *parentization* of children's play and sport. Sport is probably the best vehicle to teach values that has ever been developed. But just as a poor English teacher can prejudice a child against our great language and literature, and a poor history teacher can kill a student's interest in developing the absolutely essential knowledge of our human heritage, a poor coach can eliminate the essential values lessons that sport can teach better than any other aspect of our education system.)

EMOTIONAL DEVELOPMENT

Emotional development is enhanced by many of the areas previously covered.

Cuddling the child while feeding it or reading to it, demonstrating stable values which give the child a sense of security, and giving time to the child in the day to day activities-- all have positive effects on the emotional health of the child.

When children do not feel the security or self-respect necessary for their emotional well-being, which parents should give, there is a good chance that the child will show the effects. Juvenile delinquency, harmful drug use, failure in school, poor social development, and even early marriage can be traced to unfulfilled emotional needs. The increase in stresses, the conflicts of values, and the less personal, more automated society are held responsible for the 65 per cent increase of children being treated in mental health facilities. The same factors may be partially responsible for the high rate of suicide in the fifteen to twenty-four-year-age group. The fact that one in nine youths under nineteen has appeared before a juvenile court is also an indication of the values children hold. Somewhere along the line, the society, particularly some parents, have failed miserably in developing the emotional stability of their children.

In more primitive societies, the communities generally take more responsibility for the raising of children. But in our society the brunt of the load falls on the parents to do this enormous job. Because so many parents fail, we can certainly say that, in general, in the United States our children may be our most neglected citizens.

Most parents are quite content to change diapers for a few weeks and to show off the new baby to their friends and relatives. And most parents find many joys aiding in the development of their children. But a great many new parents seem to be counting the days until the child will be in a full-time nursery school, and the parent will be freed of the responsibility of raising the child. Recently there has been a great outcry, particularly from the feminist groups, to have publicly-paid child care centers available, so that mothers can get back into the work force where they are happier. This simple solution may relieve a parent of "feeling tied down," but there is a great deal of evidence to indicate that it may make the child feel "thrown out." It depends on the attentiveness of the care-givers at the school.

Reports from eastern Europe and the Soviet Union, before their freedom from the Communist regimes, indicated that children raised in full-time child-care centers had higher incidences of emotional disturbances, difficulties in school, and juvenile delinquency when compared with those children who had been raised at home. It appears that the problems were most pronounced among those who spent their earlier years (before they were five) in the centers.

It seems clear that if a couple wants children, there is a great need to be committed to them. It doesn't matter whether it is the mother or the father who stays home, but there must be somebody if the child is to have the best chance to feel wanted by his or her family and to be effectively socialized into that family. Having both parents in the home gives children a feeling of security and gives the children an idea of the ways a marriage can work and what roles can be played to make for a successful relationship.

There are millions of children living in broken homes. And there are millions of others who are living in families where the parents apparently don't care. Both parents may be working, be involved in outside activities, or doing so many other things that keep parents busy, busy, busy. So children can lose their parents by lack of concern as well as by divorce or death.

PSYCHOLOGICAL PARENTHOOD

Psychological parenthood is what children need. Many people assume that because two people were biologically capable of having a child, they are psychologically capable of caring for that child. But being able to perform sexual intercourse and being fertile enough to conceive a child are capabilities quite common in our species. The quality of emotional stability or the capacity to love and nurture a child, which are essential for effective parenting, are often lacking in the biological parents. Quite often too, people with the emotional abilities to be parents are sterile.

Some adult, preferably a parent, must take over the emotional development of the child. Usually this duty falls on the mother because: her hormones seem to make her more gentle; her nine months of pregnancy may give her a greater feeling of responsibility, the father is often the better income producer; and tradition has accepted the female in the "mothering" role. But in many cases men are far more competent than many women to raise their children.

Unhappily, many fathers and mothers will both abandon their duties of child raising. Sometimes it is ignorance of the needs of the child, other times it is the result of the adult being selfish. If the parents refuse to be responsible, most states have laws that can protect the child. The child can be placed with other relatives, in a foster home, or put up for adoption. But such actions are seldom taken unless the parents request it.

Many parents assume that they love their children simply because they provide for them. Nearly every animal also does this. The question is how much are we helping our children to grow independently so that they will be full-functioning adults. Since young children see the world through the lens presented by the experiences they have with their parents, it is essential that those experiences give the child the feeling of self-respect, love, and self-esteem that are necessary to function as emotionally mature adults. We know that such deprivation will have an effect on the emotional development of the child. But now there is evidence that such emotional losses may also show in stunted physical and intellectual growth. (There is evidence that the growth hormones are inhibited by a lack of parental love.)

The emotional needs of children are difficult to judge. Just as their rates of physical and intellectual growth are not exact, neither is their development of emotional maturity. Infants start life as selfish, helpless, asocial, emotional beings. The job of the parents, and later the schools, is to bring these non-socialized insecure infants to a point where they are loving, independent, social, and intellectual. We can see several paths of development of which parents should be aware.

THE PATHS OF EMOTIONAL GROWTH

Growing from selfishness to love is one of the primary goals of emotional development. If the child is cared for and comes to realize that people care, self-respect will develop. From this basis of self-respect, the ability to love will grow. Of course, obstacles can develop along the way. Jealousy of the child toward the parent of the opposite sex (the Oedipus complex) is not uncommon during the first few years of life. The child's love of, or rather need for, the other parent is threatened. The child's selfish desire for the parent will normally be overcome as the ability to love is developed. Parents can aid the children's development of the ability to love by encouraging them to show concern for others, such as writing a thank-you note to Aunt Ann, giving to United Way, or baby-sitting for friends.

Erich Fromm wrote one of the classic books on love (The Art of Loving). He said that "we learn to love by being loved." He then suggested an evolution of the ability to love.

➢ Self love—the singular concern with self, which is the domain of infants;

➢ Recognition that others are also "selfs."

> Ability to be greatly concerned with (to be able to love unselfishly) one or a few others.

> The generalized ability to love—humanitarian love. We often see this recognized in Nobel Peace Prize winners, like Mother Theresa, Albert Schweitzer, and Bishop Tutu.

The evolution from helplessness to independence is a second path of emotional growth. The child will be taught to drink from a cup, keep the bedroom neat, and do chores around the house. Parents should begin to allow children to make decisions as they become intellectually ready. At first, it may be, "Do you want vanilla or chocolate ice cream?" Later it might be, "Do you want to go with us or stay at home?" or "Do you plan on taking Spanish or German?" As the child learns to take responsibility, more independent thinking may develop.

Models will often be selected as exhibiting life styles that will allow the child to make decisions about particular goals. Early in life the goal of being a cowboy or a firefighter may predominate. Later it may be a sports idol or an entertainment figure. If these are seen to be unachievable, the older child will probably look towards occupational fields which are compatible with its developing interests and academic aptitudes.

A third pattern of emotional growth is found in **the asocial to social progression**. The infant has no social concept. Soon a relationship will be developed with one or both parents. Next it is normal to learn to play alone while sitting near another child who is also playing alone. The next stage of social growth is playing together with a friend of the same sex, then a group of friends of the same sex. Generally by age eight, groups of children will play together. Larger groups of the same sex (gangs or clubs) may develop in the teenage years. In the early teenage years, an interest in sexual relationships develops. The eventual goal of this path of development is to be at ease with all people. With this end in view, parents should not only attempt to expose their children to the appropriate groups of children, but should also be aware of their need to be able to be at ease with adults. Parents who hide their children from adult company, telling them to "go downstairs and watch the TV, " may not be doing the most they can to aid in the child's socialization. Without adequate socialization, the child will probably be introverted and lacking in a feeling of adequacy in this area.

A fourth area of concern is the **emotional to intellectual continuum.** A newborn child has only emotions. It can express fear and a few other reactions which are not unlike animals. But the child has the potential to become a being able to make decisions based on evidence. The human brain is uniquely capable of acquiring facts and feelings that can then be viewed from a variety of perspectives and can form the evidence from which decisions are made. In order to make the child's mind ready to assimilate knowledge the child will have to learn to listen, to speak, to read, and to count. Making decisions which are based on the best evidence (the scientific method) is one of the important skills to be mastered in this area of development.

This is not an all-inclusive list of emotional tasks which the child on the path to mature adulthood must master. These broad goals can be further divided. For example, we could look at the broad range of activities from the simplest to the complex. We could explore "learning to count to learning advanced calculus" or a "learning the alphabet to writing a book." But it would take several more books to expand on the possibilities.

These different experiences which a child may be given are not totally independent. For example, developing physical skills such as drinking from a cup, walking, riding a bicycle, and serving a tennis ball are useful in developing independence and becoming more social. Learning to read could help in any of the above-mentioned areas.

You can also see that each of these areas of development may never be achieved by any one person. If Fromm is right and the ultimate ability in loving is when a person can love the whole human race, then that ultimate ability to love is seldom realized. If the objective of intellectual competence includes the ability to look objectively at the evidence and make the best decision and to become fully self-actualized people, this too is seldom achieved. It is not necessary that the parents successfully guide their children along each of these paths, only that they start them and guide them an appropriate distance for each age level.

If a child needs help in reading, the parent should provide that help. If a child needs more socialization experiences, the parent should provide the setting. If a child is not making strides toward independence, the parent should aid in that direction. Since there are no absolute guidelines as to what should be done each month for each child, the parent is left to his or her own devices. The concerned parent can look at the evidence available, then do the best job possible--realizing that there has probably never been a perfect parent. *"Thank goodness! For a while it looked like the pressure was really on, didn't it?"*

There will be apparent failures along the way. Your four-year-old may become quite stubborn and maybe throw a temper tantrum. Don't worry, it's all part of the "becoming independent" path. And when your 13-year-old would rather go camping with friends than go to Hawaii with you, she's just showing some independence. And that's what you want as a parent. But if your 16-year-old elopes with the plumber, there may be a problem, because eloping is not the best method of showing independence.

MASLOW'S HIERERARCHY OF MOTIVATION

Abraham Maslow began his life as a behaviorist psychologist. As he matured, however, he became a humanist--thinking that humans are quite different from others in the animal kingdom. He looked at us as having several levels of motivations. As we satisfy one level we are ready to go to the next stage in humanness. Many of the ideas of others, like Freud's idea of sexuality, and Adler's idea that we have a need for power over ourselves and our world, can be found at different levels of Maslow's 'hierarchy of needs.'

Maslow wrote that the most basic drives are physiological. If we are not satisfied, our whole being pursues them. For example, if I am very hungry or very thirsty the desire to satisfy these basic needs will take precedence over any other desires I might have. Once these most basic needs are met my next need is safety. If I feel physically and emotionally safe I then would want love. If I am loved, the next most important need is esteem, such as the recognition of others. I can then pursue the highest human needs, those of 'self-actualization.' These needs Maslow called the *meta* needs. '*Meta*' is from the Greek word meaning 'highest.'

SELF-ACTUALIZATION (Meta needs--Morality, creativity, spontaneity, problem solving, lack of prejudice, acceptance of facts).

^ ESTEEM (Belonging, self-esteem, confidence, achievement, respect of others, respect by others.)

^ LOVE (Friendship, family, intimacy.)

^ SAFETY (Security of body, of employment, of resources, of morality, of the family, of health, of property.)

^ PHYSIOLOGICAL (Breathing, food, water, sex, sleep, homeostasis, excretion)

The physiological need for air is accomplished without even thinking about it. We don't have to say to ourselves 'inhale, exhale.' It is done unconsciously. Hunger pangs develop unconsciously but our conscious mind picks up the signal and says, 'I'm hungry.' The erection of the penis or the lubrication of the vulva occur unconsciously, usually after the conscious mind says 'I want to make love.' We can see some similarities with Freud's ideas here.

The need for safety comes next up the hierarchy. If Tarzan has satisfied his needs for food and water he may build a tree house for his safety. However, if he is very hungry he may swim across a crocodile infested river to harvest a banana tree. An infant may seek the security of a parent's arms when encountering a threatening situation. A driver may buckle the shoulder strap because there is always the possibility of an auto accident.

I have heard that 80% of Italian men from 18 to 30 still live with their parents. I guess there is a lot of safety and security in having mama take care of you. When do they start becoming responsible for themselves and the society? Italy's tight society and strong family security run counter to the competitiveness needed in global economics. No need to fight dragons when you are safe in your castle.

Maslow's third step to mental health is the need for love and affection that can be met in the family, peer group, or in some other group in which emotional bonds are formed. The love need is aided by deep emotional ties. Maslow agrees with Fromm in his belief that a lack of love is the most commonly found reason for psychological maladjustment.

Moving to the next level we find the esteem needs that relate to a person's feelings of self-worth. If a person has been loved, it goes a long way towards helping to develop a feeling of self-respect. If a person obtains the respect and praise of other people, especially when young, there is a good chance of developing an adequate feeling of self-worth. We can see some of Adler's ideas here.

The physiological, safety, love and esteem needs are called 'basic needs' by Maslow. These needs should be easily met in any civilized society. Sadly, the love and esteem needs are not met as often as would be desirable. But if these 'basic needs' are met the individual can go on to satisfy the 'truly human needs' or as Maslow called them the 'meta needs.'

The meta needs include beauty, order, unity, justice, and goodness. When you successfully meet these needs you are 'self-actualizing' or realizing your highest self. In his later work Maslow preferred the term becoming 'fully human' to the term 'self-actualization' which he had used earlier.

While many psychologists have looked at mental illness-- then developed their theories of what mental health should be—the opposite of mental illness. Or rather, a life without the symptoms of a mental illness. (At that time, psychologists were not as aware of the genetic and epigenetic causes of the symptoms of mental illness,)

Maslow started by looking at mentally healthy people. He determined which people seemed to have their highest potentials realized, then he analyzed why they were healthy. These ideas about some people achieving at a 'truly human' level were initiated when Maslow decided to analyze two of his teachers. These two people held special places in his life. They were different. They were emotionally healthy. They were creative, happy and dynamic. After analyzing their characteristics, he began to look at other people who exhibited the highest human traits.

We can also learn much from self-actualizing, mentally healthy people. 'They have higher ceilings. They can see further. And they can see in a more inclusive and integrating way. They teach us that there is no real opposition between caution and courage, between action and contemplation, between vigor and speculation, between seriousness and high level humor ... such people feel no need to deny their deeper feelings. Indeed, it is my impression that, if anything, they tend to enjoy such experiences.

You can guess that developing children who are 'truly human' is a tall order for parents. We certainly don't expect every parent to raise a truly self-actualized child, but it should be a goal. We should give every assistance possible for this to happen—and it happens more than you might imagine.

Are any of these ideas important—or even essential, for parents in today's world?

CHILD ABUSE

Child abuse is, unhappily, a common phenomenon. It is a crime which is seldom reported. The estimates of actual cases are as high as 4,000,000 annually. Deaths from child abuse may number as many as 2,000 in the U.S. Usually the mother is the person guilty of beating the child. The father is likely to stand by, doing nothing. When parents of obviously battered children are confronted with the evidence, they are likely to say *"He fell out of the highchair, "* or *"I was giving her a bath and the phone rang; she drowned in the minute I was gone. "* Usually the bruises on the child's body belie the parents' alibis. Sometimes the injuries and deaths are the results of a sudden uncontrollable frustration, other times they appear to be calculated cruelty and torture.

One recent case in California found that a mother and stepfather had made a four-year-old girl run around the house without stopping for two days until she died of exhaustion and from the beatings she received if she stopped running. The parents had previously served two years in jail for child abuse.

Child-abusing parents are likely to be mentally ill, alcoholics, or drug addicts. They are usually under twenty-five, but contrary to popular opinion, they may be at any economic, social, or intellectual level. They generally come from families in which they were beaten as children.

Generally child-beating parents are unable to cope with the problems of parenthood, especially a child's crying. A normal parent will most likely search for the cause of the child's crying, seeking outside help if necessary. The child abuser is more likely to yell at the child to "stop crying" even if the child is only a few months old. They also are likely to expect too much from a child. They may begin disciplining when the child is only three or four-months-old and may begin toilet training at six to eight months, long before the child is physiologically ready to be trained.

Nearly all parents are pushed beyond their endurance at some time. Nearly all parents will find it necessary to spank their children at some time. Both are normal. But if the parent loses control and the spanking becomes a beating, both the parent and the child become losers. The beaten child is a likely candidate for becoming maladjusted and eventually may behave as he or she has been treated--and another child beater is developed.

Now that society has recognized the extent and the severity of the problem, laws are being passed to require teachers and doctors to report incidents of abuse. Counseling centers are being expanded. Self-help groups, such as Parents Anonymous, are springing up all over the country. If you have been beaten as a child, it is quite possible that you might become a child abuser. You might well consider counseling before marriage, and you should give some consideration and study to the idea of being an effective parent.

Sexual abuse of children. We find sexual abuse in every area of life. Parents, stepparents, teachers, coaches, neighbors and others are often found to be sexual predators and abusers. We now find that in other parts of the world, parents are often selling their children into slavery and prostitution. Men are traveling to distant countries to have paid sex with children. Some children are forced into sexual situations then are videoed and exposed to the world. As caring parents we must guard against such actions against our own children and to work to prevent it with other children.

AND SO

Is this what we want for our children—abuse, neglect, experiencing hate?? Can parent licensing reduce this scourge while reducing the population and reducing warming? We know that it will probably never happen—BUT IT SHOULD! How important is our survival? How important are our children?

ONWARD!

If it's true, like Toynbee said, that 'civilizations don't have to die—because they are not organisms, but rather products of wills'—then we have a chance.

– But the civilizations that he studied died. his life mission was to study 'why.'

But no civilization of the past has faced the threat that our whole species faces today. Maybe a few can realize that many people are living beyond the means that the planet can suppo, but can enough of the world's population see it, believe it, and start to do the drastic things needed to make it happen?

➤ Nature won't clear up the mess we have caused. We have to do it. We must find ways to reduce the greenhouse gases we produce and somehow store those we have produced.

➤ I think you guys should do it. I still want my Humvee which gets 6 miles to the gallon. I want speed and power.

➤ I want air conditioning in my twelve room house and in my car.

The realities are that most people don't want to sacrifice. Just look at the American personal debt. The average Americans not only want to have everything he or she already has, they want every one of the latest gadgets, cars, video games, and home appliances that is advertised. And they want it now!

They want the homes they can't afford—and the second home they can't afford. They want the boat they can't afford and the vacation they can't afford. There are so many living in a plastic card dream world—and it usually becomes a nightmare. Do you think that these people are willing to sacrifice anything? No matter how minor?

It's a self-centered morality that generally predominates over what's good for society or even what's good for themselves in the future. Eat, drink and be merry, for tomorrow we die—or go bankrupt. Look at the number of bankruptcies and home mortgage foreclosures of a few years ago. Home owners couldn't make their house payments. The mortgage lenders went bankrupt. The stock market dropped. Everything financially is inter-related. Our planet is in a worse condition than the home mortgage lenders. But the world can't declare bankruptcy. Either we live or we die. We won't get a second chance like an over-mortgaged home owner has.

But it depends on such things as the number of trees and other plants in the world and how much more CO_2 the ocean can absorb. It has been absorbing about half of the human produced CO_2 up to now. But as the ocean warms the CO_2 is held closer to the surface and the amount of gas that can be absorbed by the whole ocean is reduced.

Then there is the fact that when the climate warms, the plants don't absorb as much carbon dioxide, probably because they reduce their growing rate so that they can conserve water. So, CO_2 emissions are not being handled as well as they were a hundred years ago. But there's more to the mix. As the world warms, there is some evidence that the tree line is rising in the northern latitudes and in the higher altitudes. But then there are some other negatives like tree damaging insects that increase as the climate warms. The average temperature is expected to increase by almost one and a half degrees Celsius by 2050. It may not sound like much but on a global scale it is immense. If we do nothing, the Earth's temperature will probably rise 4 degrees Celsius this century.

Shall we work to stop it?

ARE WE UP TO THE CHALLENGE?